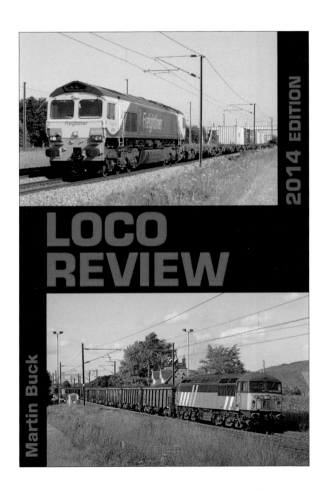

LOCO REVIEW

2014 EDITION

Martin Buck

FREIGHTMASTER

PUBLISHING

Contents

Published, December 2013 :

Freightmaster Publishing
158 Overbrook
SWINDON
SN3 6AY

www.freightmasterpublishing.co.uk

ISBN : 978-0-9558275-7-0

Printed By :

Stephens & George
Goat Mill Road
Dowlais
MERTHYR TYDFIL
CF48 3TD

www.stephensandgeorge.co.uk

Cover Images : No.66504 (top) sports its new Powerhaul livery as it passes Marholm, near Peterborough, on 6th July with 4E49, Ipswich - Scunthorpe freightliner. **Nigel Gibbs**

Ex-Fastline No.56301 (bottom) passes Ulgham Lane Crossing on 4th July with 6K61, Butterwell -Thoresby coal. **Martin Cook**

Opposite : No.56113 is back in traffic and, with No.47739 inside as insurance, heads 6E07, Washwood Heath - Boston Docks steel empties at Chellaston on 7th October. **Jamie Squibbs**

Note : All dates are 2013, unless otherwise stated.

Setting the Scene

Welcome to *Loco Review - 2014*, which devotes more pages and more images to cover the 'big' stories, such as the freight diversions put in place as a result of the Hatfield landslide and closure of both Didcot and Cockenzie power stations. Unfortunate as these closures may be, it has provided an excellent opportunity to look through the archives and find some nostalgic images of 27s, 37s, 56s, 58s and 60s working MGR coal trains.

Could 2013 be "Year of the Grid".... the Class 56 renaissance gathers pace, with more locos in traffic working more timetabled freight services. After all, it's 10-years since their withdrawal by EWS and no one could have foreseen their dramatic return to traffic.

Both Colas Rail and Devon & Cornwall Railways demonstrate their faith in the Class 56, by using these sturdy workhorses to haul timetabled services and hiring them to other freight operators when loco shortages arise.

It is worth taking a moment to highlight some flows, 56s have been engaged on:

- Chirk timber (4 flows)
- Boston steel
- Didcot Flyash
- Willesden Spoil
- Butterwell Coal
- Grangemouth Fuel Oil

All these are illustrated in this edition of *Loco Review*.

As well as exciting new freight flows, like biomass to Ironbridge power station, for example, there's a lot more to bring you:

- **Class 48s** : A celebration of 50 years of the Class 47 by illustrating the five members (Nos 47114 to 47118) which were once classified Class 48.

- **'Out of Gauge' trains** : A detailed look at what necessitates a train to run under 'out of gauge' reporting restrictions, with a '**X**' headcode.

- **Colour Changes** : All the new loco liveries and a profile of the GBRf Class 66/7s named after famous football clubs.

- **Classic Traction** : 80 pages of superb Class 20, 37, 56 and 60 action.

Finally, my thanks go to the photographers who contribute their superb images for this book, without which this title would not be possible - you are really appreciated!

Now, without further ado, please turn the page and see for yourself what makes the UK rail scene so interesting for enthusiasts and professionals alike.

Martin Buck

DIDCOT FLY ASH

Background

In October 2012, a new flow starts involving the removal of fly ash from Didcot power station to the landfill site at Calvert in Buckinghamshire. The flow is of particular note as traction will be in the shape of a DCR Class 56 (hired in by DBS) and will be routed via the Oxford - Bicester - Bletchley line.

Consist

On 26th October 2012, a DBS Class 66/0 loco hauls DCR Class 56 No.56312 and a rake of 20 'MBA" (monster) bogie boxes from Doncaster to Didcot in readiness for the start of operations.

The consist is:

500003	500131	500042	500157	500096	500094	500109	500135	500019	500093
500067	500091	500012	500081	500122	500085	500066	500148	500132	500051

Route

6Z92, 18:12 Didcot p.S. - Calvert

Didcot Power Station	**18:12 (depart)**
Foxhall Junction	18:15
Didcot North Junction	18:17
Kennington Junction	18:24
Kennington Goods Loop	18:25 - 18:34
Oxford	**18:39**
Oxford North Junction	18:50
Bicester London Road L.C.	19:10 - 19:12
Claydon L.N.E. Junction	19:36 - 19:58
Calvert	**20:28 (arrive)**

Out & About with 6Z91

Due to the late timings for the loaded fly ash service (6Z92) from Didcot power station to Calvert, photographs are mostly restricted to the returning empties from Calvert and a few are reproduced here.

Charndon : Having previously failed on the Monday, Class 56 No.56312 is now coupled up to ex-Fastline No.56301 (above), both locos producing voluminous clouds of smoke, as the train approaches Charndon on Tuesday, 4th December 2012. It departed from Claydon L&NE Junction at 11:27hrs, a few minutes earlier than the booked time, but was, however, 24 hours late as No.56312 failed the day before, having only got as far as Claydon with the empties from Calvert to Didcot.

Just like old times, a 'Grid' on the Oxford main line .... running much nearer to the booked time, No.56312 (opposite) passes Culhamn station at 12:31hrs on 7th November 2012 with 6Z91, 10:55 Calvert - Didcot power station empty flyash train, formed of 'MBA' (Monster) box wagons. These wagons were ordered by EWS during late 1998 from Thrall Europa at York to fulfil the need for large capacity box wagons capable of conveying stone, coal and scrap metal. This wagon is, effectively, a large 'MEA' and one single 'MBA' can carry just over two and a half times more than one 'MEA'.   **Geoff Plumb (2)**

Tub's Crossing, Bicester :

On 22nd November 2012, No.56312 (left) is seen passing Milepost 19, half-a-mile north of Bicester Town railway station on the Oxford - Bicester - Bletchley line with 6Z91, the 10:55 Calvert - Didcot power station flyash empties.

The '56' is on single track, which runs for over 30 miles from Oxford North Junction to Bletchley Flyover Junction.

The flyash trains access the landfill site at Calvert via a reversal at Claydon L.N.E. Jct.

Wolvercote : DCR No.56312 (top right) continues to work the loaded fly ash train (6Z92) and the return (6Z91) empties. This is 6Z91 and, amidst some nice autumnal colours, the train is seen emerging from Wolvercote Tunnel on 14th November 2012. Wolvercote Tunnel is 145 yards in length.

Calvert : After an empty trial run over the previous night/day, 6Z92 runs loaded for the first time on 30th October 2012 from Didcot to Calvert and is duly unloaded on the morning of Wednesday, 31st October. Now returning as 6Z91, No.56312 (bottom right) is 'clagging' nicely as it departs from Calvert at 10:49hrs.

Oxford Banbury Road : Mendip Rail Class 59/0 No.59005 'Kenneth J. Painter' (below) stands at Oxford Banbury Road stone terminal on 30th November 2012 after unloading, waiting departure time with 7C54, the 13:06 empties to Whatley. As luck would have it, DCR No.56312 is passing with 6Z91.   **Geoff Plumb (4)**

56312

56091

Class 56 No.56091 (above) becomes the latest member of the Class to work the Didcot to Calvert flyash train on 3rd April when, after several days of the train being cancelled, it finally works the loaded 6Z92, 18:10 Didcot power station - Calvert. It is seen here slowly negotiating the relief line at Hinksey in poor light, which did at least allow a reasonable shot from the east side of the line.   **Martin Loader**

Eight days later, 11th April, No.56091 (below) is still on the diagram and is seen passing Oxford North Junction in poor light again with 6Z91, the 10:53 Calvert - Didcot power station flyash empties.   **Mark Pike**

56303

Here it comes, emerging from amongst the trees ....

DCR No.56303 (right) is out working 6Z91, the 10:53 Calvert - Didcot flyash empties on 9th January and is seen here passing Wendlebury, south of Bicester, approaching the bridge under the M40 motorway.

The photo is shot from a public footpath across the line. **Geoff Plumb**

No.56303 (below) rounds the curve at Islip on 26th April with 6Z91 flyash empties. No apologies for yet another picture of this train, as Devon & Cornwall Railway's involvement is only temporary, following the closure of Didcot power station.

This location, at Mill Lane level crossing, has recently been cleared of vegetation in readiness for the Oxford to Bletchley route upgrade. **Martin Loader**

(Overleaf) :

Bowled! Some photographers would bemoan the passing of another train to impair the shot, however, I believe this adds to the interest. On 9th January, just as No.56303 (Page 10) heads south at Hinksey, Oxford, with 6Z91, a freightliner passes in the opposite direction, casting shadows towards the '56' and its rake of 'MBAs', three of which are still loaded. **Steven King**

On 19th March, No.56303 (Page 11) passes Didcot North Junction with 6Z91, 11:53 Calvert - Didcot power station flyash empties, whilst A1 Peppercorn 4-6-2 Pacific No.60163 'Tornado' passes in the other direction with the 08:45hrs Paddock Wood - Worcester Shrub Hill 'Cathedrals Express'. **Mark Pike**

'Tesco Express' reverts to DRS

4S43, 06:17 Daventry - Mossend   4M48, 18:53 Mossend - Daventry

November 2012 sees the 'Tesco Express' back in DRS hands and 'booked' for double-headed DRS Class 66/4 traction, in order to keep to Class 92 timings. However, this position lasts until October 2013, when DRS switch traction and hire in a Class 92 from DBS to work these trains in an attempt to get better time-keeping.

(Top Left) : The impressive looking 'Malcolm'-liveried No.66434 leads ex-Fastline No.66301 as it passes Ravenstruther, near Carstairs, on 18th January, with 4S43, the 06:17 Daventry - Mossend.   **Guy Houston**

(Bottom Left) : On a crisp winter afternoon (2nd February 2013) Nos.66423 and 66302 head across Crawford Viaduct and the infant River Clyde below with the northbound 4S43, 'Tesco Express'. **Guy Houston**

(Above) : Meanwhile, on 13th December 2012, Nos.66303 + 66427 sweep round the curve at Winwick, Warrington, with the southbound 'Tesco Express'; 4M48, the 18:53 Mossend - Daventry, running extremely late. No.66303 immaculate, having been repainted from ex-Fastline grey livery.   **Fred Kerr**

(Below) : On 24th October, now running with DBS Class 92 traction, No.92002 'H. G. Wells' has charge of 4S43 and approaches Bodsbury Crossing, just under two miles north of Beattock Summit.   **Keith McGovern**

'Tesco Express': The DRS pairing of Nos.66302 + 66426 (above) sweep through the reverse curves at Upper Denton in the Tyne Valley on Saturday, 25th May, with the diverted 4S43, 06:15 Daventry - Mossend 'Tesco Express'. This superb location is near Gilsland, north of the A69 road.   **Martin Cook**

Biomass : GBRf Class 66/7 No.66746 (below) crosses the impressive Albert Edward bridge, which spans the River Severn at Buildwas with 4V94, the 13:00 Ironbridge - Portbury empty biomass. One of Ironbridge power station's red cooling towers is partially visible   **Mike Hemming**

IRONBRIDGE BIOMASS

Background

Ironbridge is a coal fired power station capable of generating 1,000MW of electricity, located in the Severn Gorge, 0.5 miles upstream from the world heritage site of Ironbridge. The power station produces enough power to supply approximately 750,000 homes.

The station is due to close in 2015 as part of the LCPD (Large Combustion Plant Directive) as it opted out of the European Union Directive to reduce acidification, ground level ozone and particulates, by controlling the emissions of sulphur dioxide, oxides of nitrogen and dust.

Biomass

However, one generating plant at Ironbridge has been converted to use up to 100% wood pellets as a renewable fuel source, although retaining the flexibility to operate with up to 20% coal with the wood pellets, to allow most efficient operation. Initially, the biomass is imported through the Port of Tyne and the reporting details are:

6M17	00:05	Tyne Dock - Ironbridge p.s.	GBRf 66
6M09	03:25	Tyne Dock - Ironbridge p.s.	GBRf 66

Route

Interestingly, 6M17 runs (overnight) via Diggle and 6M09 runs via the Calder Valley, Copy Pit and the WCML, whilst the returning 'empties' run:

- 4E04, Ironbridge - Tyne Dock   via WCML, Shap and Hexham*
- 4E05, Ironbridge - Tyne Dock   via WCML, Copy Pit and Calder Valley.
* 4E04 via Copy Pit on Saturday.

Tyne Coal Terminal	**03:25 (depart)**	Boldon North Junction	03:39
Boldon East Junction	03:42	**Sunderland**	**03:56**
Hartlepool	04:21	Norton East Junction 04:35	
Stockton	04:42	Eaglescliffe	04:49
Boroughbridge Road L.C.	05:18	Thirsk	05:31
York	**06:18**	Colton Junction	06:26
Church Fenton	06:33	Milford Junction	06:44
Castleford	07:08	Normanton	07:25
Wakefield Kirkgate	**07:31 - 07:33**	Horbury Junction	07:44 - 07:55
Mirfield	08:15	Brighouse	08:26
Sowerby Bridge	08:37	Hebden Bridge	08:45
Hall Royd Junction 08:53		Copy Pit	09:06
Rose Grove	09:15	**Blackburn**	**09:39 - 10:07**
Lostock Hall Junction	10:20	Farington Junction	10:23
Wigan North Western	10:46	**Warrington Bank Quay**	**11:05 - 11:07**
Acton Grange Junction	11:17 - 11:49	Crewe	13:13
Norton Bridge	13:43	**Stafford**	**13:49**
Penkridge	13:57	Bushbury Junction	14:08
Stafford Road Junction	14:13	Cosford	14:21
Madeley Junction	14:29	**Ironbridge Power Station**	**14:56 (arrive)**

(Opposite) :

On 19th February, GBRf Class 66/7 No.66709 'Sorrento' passes Stirchley, south of Telford, on the Ironbridge branch with 6M09, the 03:25 Tyne Dock - Ironbridge loaded biomass.   **Mike Hemming**

Ironbridge 'B' Power Station (above) looking south from Strethill in the Ironbridge gorge.

Construction started in 1963, prior to which an 'A' power station opened in October 1932, partially closing in October 1980 with electricity generation ceasing altogether in 1981; the station was demolished in 1983.

Architect Alan Clark worked closely with landscape architect Kenneth Booth, to ensure the power station merged as much as possible into its surroundings. In this respect, the power station is hidden by wooded hills when viewed from Ironbridge and the cooling towers were constructed using concrete with a red pigment, to blend with the colour of the local soil. **Mike Hemming**

4V94 : In February, biomass train services start running out of Portbury Dock to Ironbridge (6M95). This view shows No.66746 (below) returning from the power station, having left Westerleigh Junction and is now running along the embankment at Ram Hill, CoalPit Heath, heading towards Bristol Parkway station. This is 4V94, the 10:15 Ironbridge - Portbury. **Edward Gleed**

Over The Arches

Coalbrookdale Viaduct : Viewed from the top of Strethill, looking down to Coalbrookdale viaduct, No.66711 (above) is seen passing over the 275 yards long viaduct on 20th April in charge of 6G60, the 13:27 Ellesmere Port - Ironbridge loaded biomass. This particular viaduct was constructed by Thomas Bouch between 1850-1899 and is a brick-built, twenty six-arched, structure that lies close to the cast iron Albert Edward Bridge and alongside the original Abraham Darby furnaces.   **Mike Hemming**

Lydgate Viaduct : Freight using the Copy Pit route is always welcome and on 28th February, No.66715 'Valour' (below) is seen crossing Lydgate viaduct with 6M09, two miles after leaving the Calder Valley main line at Hall Royd Junction with train 6M09.   **Neil Harvey**

In the Calder Valley

On 19th February, you can almost feel the cold air so early in the morning and when the sun is not yet high enough to shed some sunshine on No.66709 'Sorrento' (above) as it passes Dover Bridge, Eastwood, with 6M09, the 03:35 Tyne Dock - Ironbridge biomass. For some five miles between Hebden Bridge and Todmorden, the railway shares the valley with the A646 road and the Rochdale Canal.

Two days later, No.66703 'Doncaster PSB 1981-2002' (below) leaves the Calder Valley main line at Hall Royd Junction to start the climb to Copy Pit with 6M09 ex-Tyne Dock. Copy Pit summit lies 749ft above sea level and, until steam finished in August 1968, a banking engine was needed to assist freight trains over the summit in both directions, usually a Class 8f 2-8-0 from Rose Grove shed, Burnley.   **Neil Harvey (2)**

Coalbrookdale

On 7th May, 6G60, the 13:27 Ellesmere Port - Ironbridge loaded 'IIA' hoppers is running a little early tonight and No.66733 (above) runs down hill past Cherry Tree Hill, Coalbrookdale, with more biomass fuel for Ironbridge. The vantage point for this super image is a footbridge which leads from Cherry Tree Hill Road to School Road in Coalbrookdale.

Flanked on either side by silver birch trees, No.66716 'Locomotion & Carriage Institution 1911-2011' (below) ambles along the branch to Ironbridge power station, passing Madeley Court on 4th February with 6M09 loaded biomass hoppers from Tyne Dock. **Mike Hemming (2)**

HATFIELD LANDSLIDE

Background

On 12th February 2013, a major landslide takes place, which affects the railway near Hatfield and Stainforth Station, near Doncaster, in South Yorkshire.

The landslide occurred in a spoil heap at Hatfield Main Colliery, distorting a large section of the Doncaster to Goole / Scunthorpe lines. Apparently, a driver reported a "rough ride" on this section of track on 9th February, which was the first indication of the impending problems.

Consequently, all lines are blocked and **all services** running via Hatfield & Stainforth between Doncaster / Wakefield / ECML and Scunthorpe / Goole are affected.

Work to rebuild the damaged section takes five months to complete.

Diversions

The line is an important trunk freight route, with the majority of trains to and from Scunthorpe / Immingham routed that way, so numerous diversions have been put in place to reroute trains around the blockage. Basically:

Coal trains from Immingham to the Aire Valley Power stations are mainly diverted via Brigg, Gainsborough and Doncaster, with a few booked via Lincoln.

Steel trains from Scunthorpe to Lackenby are diverted via Barnetby (reverse), Brigg, Doncaster and Askern.

Trains 4O26 / 4E26 between Scunthorpe and Dollands Moor are diverted via Barnetby (reverse) and Lincoln, then direct to Newark.

6D03, Tinsley - Immingham along with 6M99, Immingham - Wolverhampton (and 6E08 return) are diverted via Brigg.

'Binliners' to & from Roxby (6M05 / 6E06) are diverted via Barnetby (reverse), Lincoln, Gainsborough and Doncaster.

Petroleum products from Lindsey to Jarrow, Preston, Neville Hill and Ferrybridge are diverted via Brigg, Gainsborough and Doncaster.

6E72 Stalybridge - Immingham is also routed via Brigg.

'Rails' from Scunthorpe to Doncaster / Eastleigh are diverted via Barnetby (reverse) and Brigg.

Re-opening

The line reopens to traffic (as planned) at 05:00hrs on Monday, 8th July.

The first train through is 6E07, Guide Bridge - Roxby empty 'binliner' at 05:05hrs (eastbound) and the first train heading west is 4L87, Scunthorpe - Ipswich containerised steel.

Apparently, inclusive of passenger services, around 40 trains traverse the reopened line by 10:00hrs, giving plenty of opportunity for the new track to bed-in!

Ante, Post Hatfield

(Above) : In happier times, this is the view prior to the landslide. Class 20 No.20301 heads east on 7th November 2012 with 3S13, Wrenthorpe - Grimsby water cannon service.   **Alan Padley**

(Opposite) : Aerial view of the affected area at Hatfield.   **Network Rail**

(Below) : The aftermath ....   **Alan Padley**

Bessacarr Diverts

Doncaster Station - Bessacarr - Gainsborough - Brigg / Lincoln - Barnetby

4D08 : Apart from freight for Goole and Hull, all other freight services travelling to Scunthorpe and Immingham are being diverted from Doncaster to Gainsborough, bringing a variety of traction and commodity to this line. On 25th March, DBS Class 66/0 No.66213 (above) slowly approaches Bessacarr Junction with empty 'HTA' bogie coal hoppers, running as 4D08, Drax power station - Immingham.

6D03 : The Tinsley - Immingham steel train is always worth a photograph, as this service uses the unique 'BVA' bogie steel flat wagons, fitted with 'cassettes' on which the steel is placed for quick loading and unloading. On 23rd March, the snow lies crisp and all around as 'shed' No.66083 (below) passes Bessacarr with the diverted 6D03, 13:45 Tinsley - Immingham loaded steel.

6E32, Preston Docks - Lindsey

On 15th March, No.66168 (above) trundles along the 'Down/Up Slow' line at Bridge Junction, Doncaster, heading for Bessacarr with 6E32, the diverted 08:55 (MWFO) Preston Docks - Lindsey empty bitumen tanks, which are still looking remarkably clean, having been introduced in November 2010.

Meanwhile, DBS Class 60 No.60063 (below) passes over some rather uneven track at Hayfield on 22nd February with ten 101.6 tonne 'ICA' bogie tank wagons in tow. **Alan Padley (4)**

25

6D49 : After being diverted via Bessacarr, freight travels via Gainsborough and thence Brigg or Lincoln for the run to Barnetby. Off its normal beaten track, No.66023 (above) passes through Gainsborough Lea Road on 17th April with the diverted 6D49, 13:55 Ferrybridge - Lindsey empty fuel oil tanks.

6D80 : It's all a bit of a blur .... on 17th April, Class 60 No.60059 'Swinden Dalesman' (below) is seen through the exhaust haze of an Eggborough bound coal train, while working 6D80, the 14:02 Neville Hill - Lindsey empty fuel oil tanks. The train is passing Beckingham signal box, two miles from Gainsborough Trent Junction, where the train will leave the Lincoln main line and head for Brigg.   **Alan Padley (2)**

6M05 : The GMC 'Binliners' are also routed via Bessacarr, thence Lincoln and a reversal at Barnetby. No.66953 (above) heads west at Bessacarr on 18th February with 6M05, the 09:30 Roxby - Northenden empty 'bins', which will resume its normal route after Doncaster at Adwick Junction.   **Alan Padley**

6E06 : After being routed through the Hope Valley, the last loaded 'GMC' binliner from Bredbury (6E06, 08:48 Bredbury - Roxby) to be diverted, runs on Friday, 5th July. Here, it passes Ferry Boat Lane Crossing, Old Denaby, hauled by FHH loco No.66419 (below); the blue livery of former operator DRS goes well with the blue waste boxes. The following Monday it will take the normal route via Diggle and the Calder Valley, then through Hatfield and Stainforth after the line re-opens.   **Derek Holmes**

Kirton Lime Sidings

The Barnetby - Brigg - Gainsborough line only sees an irregular Saturday Only passenger service, except when freight diversions are in place, like for Hatfield.

(Left) : On 19th April, GBRf No.66703 'Doncaster PSB 1981-2002' approaches Gainsthorpe road bridge at Kirton Lime Sidings with 6C09, the 08:45 Immingham - Eggborough loaded coal hoppers.

(Below) : Facing the opposite direction, this is a view of DBS Class 66/0 No.66200 passing Kirton Lime Sidings signal box with 4R15, the 08:10 Eggborough - Immingham coal empties. Kirton tunnel is visible in the distance and Kirton Lindsey station is on the other side of the tunnel.

Also known as Central Works, the 'Blue Lias Lime and Cement Works' (which made neither Blue Lias lime nor cement!) opened here in 1882, closing in 1976, although some kilns still remain on the site. It was later called the Kirton Tunnel lime works, established where the Great Central Railway cut through the Oolite ridge.   **Alan Padley (2)**

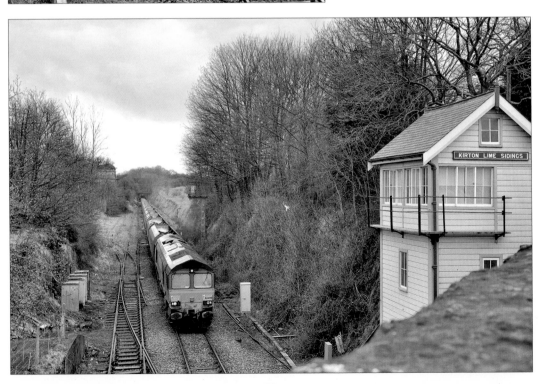

Brigg

Brigg station normally sees just three passenger trains in each direction on a Saturday. The recent landslide at Hatfield, however, has meant the line is now used by a number of re-routed freight services. Here, the old footbridge sums up the general malaise as FHH Class 66/5 No.66553 (above) accelerates through with 4R14, the 10:41 Doncaster Down Decoy - Immingham coal empties. **Syd Young**

Swinderby

This is a small village in Lincolnshire, 8 miles south-west from Lincoln and 6 miles north-east from Newark. In this quaint rural setting, No.66012 (below) approaches the gated level crossing on 19th May with 4O26, the 16:28 Scunthorpe - Dollands Moor loaded steel service, bound for Northern France. The 'shed' will join the ECML at Newark via Newark Crossing East and South Junctions. **John Binch**

Hatfield Diversions

DONCASTER (Diverted Services)

Time	Code	Train	Traction	Notes
07:05	6H16	04:32 Immingham - Drax p.s.	DBS 66	Loaded coal hoppers
07:15	6D39	05:35 Lindsey - Ferrybridge p.s.	DBS 66	Loaded bogie tanks
08:05	6Y09	05:44 Immingham - Ferrybridge p.s.	GBRf 66	Loaded coal hoppers
08:25	4E59	06:30 Ratcliffe p.s. - Hull Docks	FHH 66	Empty coal hoppers
10:00	6N31	07:16 Scunthorpe - Lackenby	DBS 66	Loaded steel
10:10	4R35	08:35 Drax p.s. - Immingham	FHH 66	Empty coal hoppers
10:55	6D79	09:00 Lindsey - Neville Hill	DBS 66 / 60	Fuel oil tanks
11:05	6C09	08:41 Immingham - Eggborough p.s.	GBRf 66	Loaded coal hoppers
12:50	6Y13	09:43 Immingham - Ferrybridge p.s.	FHH 66	Loaded coal hoppers
13:20	6M05	10:05 Roxby - Northenden R.T.S.	FHH 66	Empty GMC 'binliner'
13:30	6E32	08:55 Preston Docks - Lindsey	DBS 66 / 60	Empty bogie tanks
14:10	6J94	12:09 Hull / 12:50 Goole - Rotherham	DBS 66	Empty steel
14:45	6C44	12:50 Immingham - Eggborough p.s.	DBS 66	Loaded coal hoppers
15:05	6D49	14:13 Ferrybridge p.s. - Lindsey	DBS 66	Empty bogie tanks
15:50	6D80	14:20 Neville Hill - Lindsey	DBS 66 / 60	Fuel oil tanks
15:50	4R37	15:04 Drax p.s. - Immingham	FHH 66	Empty coal hoppers
16:25	6R14	13:45 Immingham - Ferrybridge p.s.	FHH 66	Loaded coal hoppers
17:45	6R35	15:59 Immingham - Drax p.s.	FHH 66	Loaded coal hoppers
18:10	6D11	13:55 Lackenby - Scunthorpe	DBS 66	Empty steel
18:30	4R22	17:35 Drax p.s. - Immingham	FHH 66	Empty coal hoppers
19:30	6D43	13:50 Jarrow - Lindsey	DBS 60	Empty bogie tanks
19:50	4R30	18:22 Eggborough p.s. - Immingham	DBS 66	Empty coal hoppers
20:35	6Y21	17:45 Immingham - Ferrybridge p.s.	GBRf 66	Loaded coal hoppers
20:35	6C51	17:45 Immingham - Eggborough p.s.	GBRf 66	Loaded coal hoppers
21:10	6E72	18:22 Stalybridge - Immingham	DBS 66	Empty bogie tanks
22:55	6N73	19:44 Scunthorpe - Lackenby	DBS 66	Loaded steel

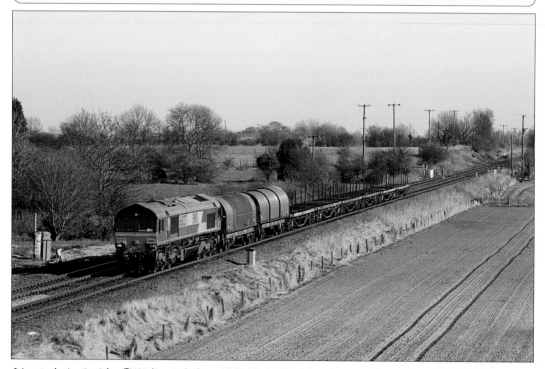

Diverted via Snaith : EWS-liveried Class 66/0 No.66027 (above) approaches Whitley Bridge Junction on 28th February with the diverted 6J94, 12:50 Hull/Goole Docks - Rotherham steel train which normally runs via Hatfield, but has come via the rarely used single line section between Goole and Snaith.   **Neil Harvey**

BARNETBY

Time	Code	Train	Traction	Notes
06:35	6E01	03:16 Northenden R.T.S - Roxby	FHH 66	Loaded GMC 'binliner'
07:15	6D74	05:46 Doncaster Decoy - Scunthorpe	DBS 66	Departmental
08:20	6N31	07:16 Scunthorpe - Lackenby	DBS 66	Loaded steel
10:15	6D75	09:18 Scunthorpe - Doncaster Decoy	DBS 66	Departmental (rails)
11:10	6M05	10:05 Roxby - Northenden R.T.S.	FHH 66	Empty GMC 'binliner'
13:40	6E06	07:45 Bredbury - Roxby	FHH 66	Loaded GMC 'binliner'
14:50	6V66	13:36 Scunthorpe - Llanwern	DBS 66	Loaded steel
15:45	4E26	07:45 Dollands Moor - Scunthorpe	DBS 66	Empty steel (ex Ebange)
17:25	4O26	16:28 Scunthorpe - Dollands Moor	DBS 66	Loaded steel
17:45	6M06	16:32 Roxby - Bredbury R.T.S.	FHH 66	Empty GMC 'binliner'
19:10	6D11	13:55 Lackenby - Scunthorpe	DBS 66	Empty steel
19:45	6E67	12:15 Llanwern - Scunthorpe	DBS 66	Empty steel

Rakes of 'HTAs' are a common sight at Heck Ings, but this is a diverted service - 4D37, 11:09 West Burton - Hull Coal Terminal, hauled by DBS-liveried No.66097 (above). This train would normally go via Hatfield but has been sent (off route) from Doncaster via Shaftholme Junction - Knottingley South and East Junctions - Snaith - Goole. In this view, the train has just passed under the ECML and the chimney at Eggborough power station looms above the line.
Neil Harvey

LINCOLN

Time	Code	Train	Traction	Notes
06:45	4L87	04:28 Scunthorpe - Ipswich Yard	FHH 66	Containerised steel
11:10	4R35	08:35 Drax p.s. - Immingham	FHH 66	Empty coal hoppers
11:20 -	6R60	09:30 Immingham - Drax p.s.	FHH 66	Loaded coal hoppers
11:55	6M05	10:05 Roxby - Northenden R.T.S.	FHH 66	Empty GMC 'binliner'
12:55	6E06	07:45 Bredbury - Roxby	FHH 66	Loaded GMC 'binliner'
15:05	4E26	07:45 Dollands Moor - Scunthorpe	DBS 66	Empty steel(ex Ebange)
15:35	4R18	14:44 Doncaster Decoy - Immingham	GBRf 66	Empty coal hoppers
17:40	4R71	16:39 Doncaster Decoy - Immingham	GBRf 66	Empty coal hoppers
18:30	4O26	16:28 Scunthorpe - Dollands Moor	DBS 66	Loaded steel (to Ebange)
18:55	6E67	12:15 Llanwern - Scunthorpe	DBS 66	Empty steel
19:05	6V19	17:26 Immingham - Margam	DBS 66	Steel / fuel oil tanks
19:20	4R22	15:35 Drax p.s. - Immingham	FHH 66	Empty coal hoppers

Barnetby

With no direct access to the main network, freight services to and from Scunthorpe have to faff around reversing at Barnetby before going where they need to be, like No.66008 (above) crossing Wrawby Junction into the down sidings on 29th March with 6N31, the 07:55 Scunthorpe - Lackenby steel. **Syd Young**

This is the rare sight of 6O73, the 12:05 Scunthorpe Redbourne Sidings - Dollands Moor (Ebange) loaded steel seen east of Barnetby on 13th April, due to the loco having to run round its train in Immingham reception sidings on this particular day. EWS-liveried No.66128 (below) passes Barnetby East with a consist of the usual steel frame fitted 'FIAs', plus six 'IGAs' behind the loco. **Neil Harvey**

A sight which may to be consigned to history, wisps of smoke gently rising into the afternoon sky from the cooling towers of Didcot power station. Will they be demolished or survive a preservation order?

Class 60 No.60007 (above) in striking Loadhaul livery is seen passing Milton, just west of Didcot, with 6C65, the 13:55 Didcot - Avonmouth MGR empties while, in the background, No.60077 heads for the power station with 6G81, the 10:45hrs loaded service from Avonmouth. This popular vantage point to view westbound train services is Milton Bridge, which can be accessed off the A34 or A4130. **Martin Buck**

Didcot 'A' - End of an Era

The News ....

Didcot 'A' Power Station stops generating electricity at 14:00hrs on Friday, 22nd March.

Background

The 2,000 megawatt (MW) coal-fired Didcot 'A' plant began operating in 1970 and had an active life of 43 years. However, it opted out of the European Union's Large Combustion Plant Directive aimed at reducing emissions and to comply it had to cease generation by the end of December 2015 at the latest.

Nine months decommissioning begins on 31st March and demolition of the six towers is expected to take several years. The station was disconnected from the national grid at 14:00 GMT and a former power station worker, Lyn Bowen, (who originally connected Didcot to the national grid in 1970) flicked the switch to disconnect.

Construction

Didcot 'A' Power Station was initially a coal fired (later, gas, as well) power station, designed by architect Frederick Gibberd, for the Central Electricity Generating Board (CEGB). Building work started on the 2,000 MW power station during 1964 and was completed in 1968 at a cost of £104m. Up to 2,400 workers were employed at peak times and the site is located on 300 acres of land, which occupies the site of a former Ministry of Defence Central Ordnance Depot. The main chimney is 650ft and there are six cooling towers, each 325ft in height.

Supply

Didcot 'A' used four 500 MW generating units and, by way of example, in 2003 it consumed 3.7 million tonnes of coal, most of which was imported through the Port of Avonmouth, brought in by rail. A sample schedule of coal trains planned to run in the final week of operations is given below, the final trainload of imported coal runs on Tuesday, 19th March.

6D17, the 14:22 Avonmouth S1 - Didcot ps   DBS Class 66/0 No.66117

DIDCOT POWER STATION
Week Commencing 18th March 2013

Arr.	Code	Train	Traction
01:30	6D01	22:47 Avonmouth - Didcot ps	DBS 66
03:37	6D03	00:59 Avonmouth - Didcot ps	DBS 66
05:13	6D05	02:16 Avonmouth - Didcot ps	DBS 66
07:30	6D07	04:54 Avonmouth - Didcot ps	DBS 66
11:37	6D11	08:27 Avonmouth - Didcot ps	DBS 66
14:39	6D13	11:00 Avonmouth - Didcot ps	DBS 66
16:01	6D15	13:24 Avonmouth - Didcot ps	DBS 66
17:50	6D17	14:22 Avonmouth - Didcot ps	DBS 66
21:38	6D21	19:01 Avonmouth - Didcot ps	DBS 66
23:32	6D23	20:53 Avonmouth - Didcot ps	DBS 66

Portfolio

To mark the passing of Didcot 'A', there now follows a special portfolio of coal traffic, dating back to the 1990s, which includes some classic traction - 56s, 58s and 60s.

Class 58 No.58006 (above) passes Thrupp (between Banbury and Oxford) with 7V44, the 09:34 Three Spires Junction - Didcot power station MGR coal train on 25th April 1986. Although difficult to tell from this picture, the cement works at Shipton-on-Cherwell was still in use at this time, but closed shortly afterwards and has lain derelict for many years, although most of the buildings and the landmark chimney still stand.

On 17th August 1988, Large Logo Class 56 No.56101 (below) passes Bletchingdon with 7V85, the 13:58 Toton New Bank - Didcot. At this time there was still a possibility of seeing Class 56s on coal trains from the Midlands to Didcot, although the majority of workings were in the hands of Class 58s.   **Martin Loader (2)**

Midlands Coal

Prior to imported coal coming on stream from Avonmouth, Didcot power station received supplies of coal from collieries in the Midlands and there could be some 14 trainloads of coal (see below) per day. The trains would be formed of the iconic 'HAA' 2-axle 'MGR' coal hopper, hauled initially by Class 47s, followed by Class 58s and the occasional '56' or '60'.

The 'HAA' was the largest fleet of air-braked wagons built for BR comprising over 11,000 32-ton Coal Hoppers introduced under the 'Merry-Go-Round' concept. The basis for these wagons was to operate in a non-stop loop from colliery to power station, both loading and unloading being undertaken while travelling at low speed. The track layout at the power station was so designed so that coal discharge could be performed without stopping or shunting. The Merry Go Round principle is still in use today, albeit utilising newer bogie hoppers.

Typical Coal Schedule - January 1988

Arr.	Code	Train		Traction
00:19	7V95,	21:43	Bescot – Didcot	Class 58
03:15	7V20,	23:51	Mantle Lane – Didcot	Class 58
04:00	7V26,	23:16	Markham Main – Didcot	Class 58
11:50	7V44,	09:42	Three Spires – Didcot	Class 58
12:50	7V49,	09:17	Baddesley – Didcot	Class 58
14:39	7V09,	08:41	Markham Main – Didcot	Class 58
15:20	7V65,	13:08	Three Spires – Didcot	Class 58
17:15	7V06,	13:54	Mantle Lane - Didcot	Class 58
18:20	7V85,	13:58	Toton – Didcot	Class 58
18:14	7V60,	15:15	Baddesley – Didcot	Class 58
20:13	7V23,	15:04	Markham Main – Didcot	Class 58
20:52	7V04,	17:04	Mantle Lane – Didcot	Class 58
22:33	7V90,	20:24	Three Spires – Didcot	Class 58
22:45	7V92,	19:25	Mantle Lane – Didcot	Class 58

Appropriately adorned with Trainload Coal decals, No.58040 'Cottam Power Station' (above) passes through Radley station on 9th July 1991 with 7V85, the 13:58 Toton - Didcot loaded MGR coal. This was in the days when Radley station was little used, with just a few cars in the car park, in contrast to today's completely full and extended car park.   **Martin Loader**

After depositing its payload of coal, No.60069 'Humphry Davy' (left) leaves Didcot power station on 20th February 1993 with the late running 6E13, 12:15 Didcot - Barrow Hill MGR empties.

The Coal Discharger at the power station (visible in the background, by the side of the leftmost cooling tower) receives trains on two discharge lines, which are on a loop of 1.82 miles in length.

The 'HAA' hopper is fitted with automechanical doors at the bottom of the wagon to enable an efficient discharge of coal.   **Martin Loader**

There are not too many pictures of Class 56s working MGR coal trains from the Midlands to Didcot power station in the 1980s at their ultimate destination. On 12th June 1983, No.56064 (above) draws slowly forward into the unloading building prior to dropping its load of coal through the slatted floor. It would move through at 0.5mph, with the wagon doors being tripped by the blue actuators on the right. **Martin Loader**

(Previous Images)

Railfreight Grey, Large Logo, No.56062 (page 38) approaches Oxford on 22nd April 1986 with 7V65, the 11:56 Desford Colliery - Didcot power station loaded MGR. It is viewed from Walton Well Road bridge, which is relatively traffic free.

Railfreight Grey liveried No.58023 (Page 39) climbs the 1 in 187 gradient past Harbury on 10th May 1989 with 7V09, the 08:41 Markham Colliery - Didcot MGR. All this is now history, No.58023 is no longer in service, nor the vintage 'HAA' wagons it is hauling. Not only has the train gone, so has the view, as a wall of trees and bushes now block out this, once iconic viewpoint.   **Martin Loader (2)**

On 2nd May 1992, No.58043 (above) rounds Didcot West Curve (between Foxhall Junction and Didcot North Junction) with 6E11, the 10:15 Didcot - Barrow Hill MGR coal empties. At the time, coal trains were the main users of this curve and the liberal additional coal 'ballast' shows that the hopper doors of the, supposedly empty, wagons obviously didn't fit too well!

A busy freight moment at Hinksey Yard, Oxford, on 8th May 1985, as No.58016 (below) heads northwards with 6M82, 16:05 Didcot - Toton MGR empties, while the crew of Class 31/1 No.31289 wait next to their loco ready to follow it with the 6M93, 16:20 Morris Cowley - Bescot 'Speedlink'. **Martin Loader (2)**

With the 'dreaming spires' of Oxford just visible at the rear of the train, No.58028 (above) passes Wolvercote with 6M06, Didcot - Daw Mill MGR empties on 10 July 1987. This really dramatic lighting didn't last long of course, as the rain which was falling over the city of Oxford, soon reached this point.

Mainline-liveried No.60074 'Braeriach' (below) slowly approaches Hallen Marsh Junction on 24 July 1996 with a loaded MGR coal train for Didcot power station. The train is just a few minutes into its journey, the loading bunker being clearly visible directly above the loco.   Martin Loader (2)

Class 56 No.56114 'Maltby Colliery' (above) stands at the recently completed Avonmouth Bulk Handling Terminal during gauging trials on 25th June 1993. Along with Class 60 No.60077 (which can just be glimpsed through the bunker in the background) and Class 37 No.37887, it was used with rakes of 'HEA' wagons for checking clearances through the new structure, prior to services of imported coal starting to Didcot power station. This saw a switch of supply for Didcot from home produced coal from the Midlands to imported coal, supposedly a 'greener' alternative due to its lower sulphur content. Although, of course, the pollution caused by transporting it halfway round the world was ignored! **Martin Loader**

Avonmouth Coal

From August 1993, MGR trains carrying imported coal started running from Avonmouth Bulk Import Terminal to Didcot power station, replacing the flows from the Midlands, albeit still utilising 'HAAs' and Class 60 traction.

This situation remained until 2001 / 2002 when EWS introduced new 'HTA' bogie hoppers, built with buckeye couplings only, with no buffers, and could only be hauled by Class 66 diesels that had swing-head buckeye couplings fitted. These '66s' were now coming on stream to replace older, non-standard, traction like 37s, 47s, 56s, 58s and even the 60s.

The new 'HTAs' had greater benefits .... a train of 19 wagons could carry 1,432 tons of coal, compared to 1,206 tons with the old 'HAA' train, and the empties from Didcot to Avonmouth could be classified as Class 4, running at 75mph.

AVONMOUTH COAL TRAINS - Sample Daytime schedule, March 2001

Code	Train		Code	Train	
6A64	07:07	Avonmouth - Didcot	6A65	08:32	Avonmouth - Didcot
6G80	09:29	Avonmouth - Didcot	6G81	10:45	Avonmouth - Didcot
6A13	12:49	Avonmouth - Didcot	6G82	14:52	Avonmouth - Didcot
6A59	15:33	Avonmouth - Didcot	6A68	16:40	Avonmouth - Didcot

The 'HAAs' were built between 1964 - 1977 at BR Darlington, Shildon and Ashford, numbered 350000 - 359571, 365000 - 366129 and 368000 - 368459 with operation in block trains of up to 35 wagons. On a glorious summer day in July 2001, Class 60 No.60077 (above) passes through Stoke Gifford with 6A65, the 08:32 Avonmouth - Didcot loaded MGR. The train is passing the purpose built Royal Mail terminal adjacent to Bristol Parkway station and, unfortunately, the terminal is no longer there as a result of the Royal Mail dispensing with mail services by rail in January 2004. **Martin Buck**

In this view, circa July 2000, an unidentified Class 60 (above) passes Highworth Junction, Swindon, with 6A65, the 08:32 Avonmouth - Didcot. In the background, Class 66 No.66161 marshals some Rover 'cube' wagons to form 4M08, 14:15 Swindon - Longbridge and another Class 60 is atop 6C67, the 10:38 Swindon - Avonmouth. At the time, MGR empties were being staged at Swindon due to limited capacity at Avonmouth.

In hazy spring sunshine in mid-March 1999, EWS-liveried No.60049 (below) passes Shrivenham with 6C64, the 11:59 Didcot - Avonmouth MGR coal empties. This road bridge and the footbridge in the background are two popular vantage points on this stretch of the main line between Didcot and Swindon.   **Martin Buck (2)**

MGR Coal Hopper Profile

During the 1990s, the 2-axle 'MGR' coal hopper was the sole type of wagon bringing coal from the Midlands and Avonmouth to Didcot power station. As can be seen from the images for this feature, both 'open' and 'hooded' types were used. Here is a breakdown of all the various types:

'HAA' : **Original 2-axle MGR Coal Hopper - 45 mph loaded / 55 or 60 mph empty.**

 Built : 1964 - 1977 by BREL Ashford / Darlington / Shildon

'HDA' : **2-axle MGR Coal Hopper, maximum speed 60 mph.**

 Built : 1980 - 1982 by BREL Shildon

'HMA' : **2-axle MGR Coal Hopper fitted with modified brake**.

 Built : 1964 - 1977 by BREL Ashford / Darlington / Shildon

'HNA' : **2-axle MGR Coal Hopper fitted modified brake and canopy.**

 Built : 1964 - 1977 by BREL Ashford / Darlington

The hoppers fitted with a canopy meant the top extension allowed a greater payload of 32 tonnes and so utilised the maximum axle weight of 22.5 tonnes per wagon. However, these canopies were only of use where the height of the colliery / loading terminal permitted their operation. They soon became damaged, with some canopies being removed altogether.

There were also three other 2-axle 'MGR' type of hoppers:

'HBA' / 'HCA' / 'HFA'

These were also fitted with a canopy and used to convey limestone from Hardendale and Shap quarry to steelworks around the country, such as Port Talbot and Redcar.

No.60087 'Slioch' (above) arrives at Didcot with 6A65, the 09:03 ex-Avonmouth loaded MGR on 29th February 1996, formed entirely of hoppers fitted with a canopy. The train is approaching Foxhall Junction and will shortly run round its train before heading into the power station.   **Martin Loader**

Foxhall Junction

The A413 road bridge overlooking Foxhall Junction provided an excellent, if not noisy and busy, vantage point to view MGR coal trains serving Didcot power station. After running round its train near Didcot Parkway station, Mainline blue liveried No.60011 (above) passes Foxhall Junction on 29th May 1997 with 6C66, the 16:09 Didcot - Avonmouth MGR empties. It will take the bi-directional line as far as Steventon.

"Brief Encounter" .... an interesting (and unique?) meeting of Class 60s on MGRs at Foxhall Junction on 13th March 1997, as each loco is in a different and temporary livery applied by the newly privatised freight companies. Loadhaul No.60064 'Back Tor' (below) approaches with 6A64 from Avonmouth, as Mainline No.60086 'Schienhallion' waits to proceed with 6C67 empties to Avonmouth. **Martin Loader (2)**

'**HTAs**' start to appear on the Avonmouth - Didcot coal circuit in 2001, hauled by EWS Class 66/0s, putting an end to Class 60-hauled 2-axle MGR hopper operations. These high-capacity bogie hoppers were built at Thrall works in York between 2001 - 2004 and a total of 1,144 'HTAs' entered traffic.

A rake of 'HTAs' on this circuit consisted of 23 wagons, as can be seen here at Bourton (east of Swindon) when No.66223 (above) was in charge of 6D15, the 08:51 Avonmouth - Didcot; the wagons are starting to lose their shine, some already vandalised by a so called graffiti artist.

When Avonmouth coal trains reach Didcot, the loco will run round in the 'Up Goods Loop' at the west end of Didcot Parkway station, in order to proceed to the power station. On 30th September 2011, No.66126 (below) is about to uncouple from 6D13, the (MFO) 11:00 Avonmouth - Didcot loaded EWS hoppers and go onto the other end of its train.   **Martin Buck (2)**

Daw Mill Supplements

While regular supplies of imported coal arrived at Didcot from Avonmouth, the power station also received occasional supplies of domestic coal from Daw Mill colliery in the Midlands:

6V37, 08:50 Daw Mill - Didcot	DBS Class 66
6Z98, 12:57 Daw Mill - Didcot	FHH Class 66

On 3rd June 2011, DBS Class 66/0 No.66184 (above) slowly eases its train of loaded 'HTAs' around Didcot West Curve heading for the Great Western Main Line at Foxhall Junction, this train service being 6V37, the 08:50 Daw Mill - Didcot power station. Meanwhile, later in the day, as shadows encroach across the running lines, FHH Class 66/6 No.66620 (below) emerges into a welcome patch of sunshine at Foxhall Junction with 6Z98, the 12:57 Daw Mill - Didcot. **Martin Buck (2)**

Tilbury Coal : May 2011 saw the start of Tilbury 'B' power station converting to biomass operation, which meant that stockpiles of surplus coal would be transferred for use at Didcot power station, via a 6V42 overnight train from Ripple Lane. This resulted in the returning empties becoming an unusual sight, and perhaps the only time 'HTAs' have been seen east of Didcot on Great Western metals. On 1st July 2011, DBS liveried No.66097 (above) heads past Cholsey Manor Farm with 4L36, 09:56 Didcot Yard - Ripple lane.

Didcot Coal Miscellany

For the record, Tilbury power station opened in 1968 and received its coal by ship, via a jetty enlarged in 2004 to accommodate ships carrying up to 65,000 tons of coal.   **Martin Buck**

Rare Power : A welcome surprise at the end of a warm summer evening at Wolvercote Junction when, instead of the staple 56 or 58 traction, Class 37/0 No.37147 (below) turns up with MGR empties, just as the sun was setting on 6th July 1987. The train is presumed to be 6M61, the 20:00 Didcot - Toton and the very last glimmers of sun give a slight pink tinge to the ballast and the A34 bridge. A rare picture of a 37, complete with original skirts and round buffers, hauling a rake of 'HAAs'.   **Martin Loader**

Another Closure ....

Cockenzie p.s.

The News ....

The 1,200 megawatt power station ceases generating energy on 15 March.

Background

The power station is situated on the south shore of the Firth of Forth, near the town of Cockenzie and Port Seton, eight miles east of Edinburgh; its two chimneys dominating the coastline since opening in 1967. The coal fired power station was forced to close under the Large Combustion Plant Directive (LCPD) and in 2005 it was cited as the UK's least carbon-efficient power station, in terms of carbon dioxide released per unit of energy generated.

The station was initially operated by the nationalised South of Scotland Electricity Board, followed by Scottish Power since privatisation in 1991. The station began generating electricity in 1968 and in 2000 - 2001, Cockenzie generated a record load factor, supplying 3,563 GWh of electricity and burning 1,500,000 tonnes of coal.

Coal Deliveries

Coal originally came from the deep coal mines situated in the Midlothian Coalfield but, following their supplies being exhausted, coal has been supplied from open cast mines in the Lothians, Fife, Ayrshire and Lanarkshire. Russian coal was used latterly due to its low sulphur content (which reduces Sulphur Oxide emissions) imported through Hunterston and Leith Docks.

For the record, Cockenzie was the first to use the 'Merry-Go-Round' system of coal deliveries by rail using 2-axle 'HAA' wagons. The first seven members of the Class 26 fleet (D5300 - D5306, later renumbered 26007, 26001 - 006 respectively) were given slow speed control apparatus in 1967 for use on MGR coal trains to the then new Cockenzie Power Station.

Last Train

The last trainload of coal into the power station, hauled by DBS Class 66/0 No.66077, was:

6B72, Hunterston - Cockenzie (loaded)
4J45, Cockenzie - Falkland Yard (empties)

No.66077 (above) has charge of the final working and is seen on 9th March approaching Prestonpans, having just left Cockenzie reception sidings to join the ECML. The train is 4J45, the 17:38 Cockenzie - Falkland Yard empties - Cockenzie RIP. **Steven Brykajlo**

Cockenzie Coal Handling Plant

Cockenzie had the capacity to hold up to 900,000 tonnes of coal in a storage bing (heap), situated beside the B6371 road and transferred by conveyor belt across the B1348 road to the power station at Cockenzie & Port Seton. The coal, at this stage, had to be weighed, sampled and screened for metal and stones before being transported to the main station and stored in bunkers.

Due to prohibited space at the unloading bunker, its two lines are not long enough and coal trains have to be split into two sections. On 2nd February, No.66528 (above) is unloading its second set of wagons after unloading the wagons to the right, off 6Z03, the 13:00 Leith Docks - Cockenzie. **Keith McGovern**

DBS and FHH at Cockenzie

All five reception lines appear to be in active use on 17th February 2007, judging by the shiny rails at Cockenzie. No.66132 (above) marshals loaded 'HAAs', having arrived with 7B03, 13:45 Leith Docks - Cockenzie, whilst the driver of No.66023 awaits departure time with 6B55, 15:42 MGR empties to Millerhill.

Now, more than five years later, the sidings are overgrown with weeds and only two lines are in use. FHH No.66598 (below) is seen on 9th October 2012 about to leave with empty FHH hoppers bound for the coal loading point at Ravenstruther. The incoming train came from Leith Docks. **Keith McGovern (2)**

From the archives ....

On a cold winter day in February 1993 (date unknown), Class 56 No.56029 (right), complete with black diamond coal sector decals on the body side, is seen slowly leaving the reception sidings with MGR empties bound for Blindwells, less than a mile away.

In the 1970s, the huge opencast coal mine was opened at Blindwells, just to the north east of Tranent, which supplied coal to Cockenzie Power Station and for export.

Coal production ceased in 2000, bringing to an end at least eight centuries of coal mining in the area. **Max Fowler**

In this 'going away' shot, two-tone grey Class 26 No,26002 (above) makes its way down the Bilston Glen branch with MGR empties from Cockenzie, to be loaded with another load of the black stuff for the power station. Bilston Glen colliery was at the end of a four mile freight-only line off Millerhill South Junction.

Bilston Glen colliery opened in 1963 and became famous as the focus of discontent in Scotland during the 1984-85 miners' strike. It closed in 1989 and was later demolished. A third colliery, Monktonhall, was situated adjacent to Millerhill Yard, despatching coal to Cockenzie, before closing in 1998. **Keith McGovern**

(Overleaf)
(Page 56) : On 26th July 1991, Class 37/5 No.37693 arrives with loaded 'HAAs' from nearby Blindwells; Cockenzie power station looms large above the train to dominate the background. **Max Fowler**

(Page 57) : Class 56 No.56123 'Drax Power Station' is seen pulling its train of 'HAA' coal wagons slowly through the MGR unloading bunker on 23rd July 1996, having originated from Blindwells opencast mine. It is difficult to appreciate from this picture, but this dead end line is situated on a high embankment, and the ground drops away sharply right behind the photographer. The power station is actually located near the Firth of Forth, some distance away from the unloading bunker. **Martin Loader**

BR Blue 26/0s ....

26007 (above) pokes its nose out into the open as it slowly leaves the power station branch and negotiates the junction to join the ECML at Prestonpans on 26th April 1983 with an empty MGR coal train en route from Cockenzie to Monktonhall Colliery. Having joined the main line, No.26007 (below) accelerates through Prestonpans station, heading for Monktonhall Junction and then via Millerhill East Junction to reach the colliery. Monktonhall Colliery was the last deep mine in the Lothians, a large and modern pit when it opened in 1953, but was plagued by flooding and closed in 1998.

26001 (above) on an unknown date, possibly early 1982, is about to leave Cockenzie power station reception sidings with a rake of empty, canopy fitted, MGR hoppers for Monktonhall.

26005 (below) sweeps round the curve at Monktonhall Junction, in the southern suburbs of Musselburgh, heading for Cockenzie power station in August 1982 with loaded hoppers from Monktonhall. Please don't shoot the messenger, but the 26 in this image may not be number 5!

The Haymarket Class 26s, No.26001 - 26007, were all given slow speed control apparatus in 1967 for use on MGR coal trains to the then new Cockenzie power station. **Keith McGovern (4)**

Sottish Coal in Administration

News ....

Scottish Coal cuts 590 jobs at mines in Ayrshire, Lanarkshire and Fife

Background

April comes with the announcement that 600 people have been made redundant, following the collapse of one of Scotland's biggest coal-mining companies, Scottish Coal; six open cast mines in East Ayrshire, South Lanarkshire and Fife have stopped production.

Apparently, falling coal prices and rising operational costs have been blamed for causing losses and "significant cash flow pressures".

Ravenstruther coal loading point, also known as 'Renstrie', is located just north of Carstairs, on the 'Down' side of the WCML. It receives coal from the open-cast mines in and around the Douglas Basin, South Lanarkshire.

In the early 1990s, a new loading bunker was built to cater for increased coal supplies, especially export through Ayr Harbour, before extending operations to Cockenzie and Longannet power stations. Anglo-Scottish flows soon followed, Drax power station, in particular, being a major recipient.

Railfreight Casualties

The two loading points affected are Ravenstruther (Lanarkshire) and Killoch (Ayrshire) and at the time of the announcement, the following train services ceased running:

6G05,	09:29	Ravenstruther - Longannet	6M65,	13:56	Ravenstruther - Ratcliffe
6Z71,	16:55	Ravenstruther - Ratcliffe	6G20,	19:01	Ravenstruther - Longannet
6M11,	04:38	Killoch - Fiddlers Ferry (TX)	6E73,	04:38	Killoch - Drax (TO)
6Z68,	07:02	Killoch - Drax (MTX)	6E74,	18:57	Killoch - Drax
6E94,	23:45	Killoch - Drax			

As a consequence, Anglo-Scottish coal flows will now originate from Hunterston (imported), Greenburn and New Cumnock.

Ravenstruther : On the second day of Class 60 operation at Ravenstruther, 12th May 1992, No.60091 'An Teallach' (above) runs its wagons through the loading tower in readiness for a run to York, where the train will be staged before going on to an Aire Valley power station. The two-tone grey 60 carries Trainload Coal decals of black & yellow squares with black diamonds. **Max Fowler**

Super power .... double-headed 56s became a regular sight in the early '90s on MGRs leaving Ravenstruther. On 1st May 1991, No.58083 + No.56112 (above) approach Carstairs, destined for Millerhill with a loaded MGR. **Keith McGovern (2)**

Many MGR sets and locos were staged at Millerhill and Nos.56073 + 56082 (middle) are seen running light through the yard in readiness for their next turn of duty.

June 2005 : It's busy at Ravenstruther. Following the failure of Class 66/0 No.66113, parked in the Cripple Siding, sister loco No.66176 (below) arrives from Mossend to take over its duties. A rake of 'HTA' coal hoppers waits to be taken through the loading bunker. **Max Fowler**

Killoch

Killoch Colliery closed in 1987, but the railhead remained intact and became a distribution centre by Scottish Coal, as a coal washery and blending plant. It was on a single track branch, four miles from Annbank Jct. and processed and despatched a variety of coal products:

Product	Flow	Wagons Used
Coal Slurry	Killoch to Methil P.S.	2-axle 'SSA' wagons
Export Coal	Killoch - Ayr Harbour	2-axle 'HAA' MGR hoppers
Domestic Coal	Killoch - Blackburn / Shrewsbury	2-axle 'HEA' wagons
Industrial Coal	Killoch - Ketton Cement Works	2-axle 'MEA' wagons
Coal	Killoch - Cockenzie / Longannet	2-axle 'HAA' MGR hoppers
	Killoch - English Power Stations	Bogie 'HHA'/ 'HTA' Bogie Hoppers
Washing & Blending	Various	Various

'HAAs' : A mechanical digger (right) is in the process of loading a rake of 2-axle 'HAA' coal hoppers.

At the time, a Motherwell Class 08 shunter (No.08411) was out-based at Killoch Washery to manoeuvre coal wagons on site.

Two-tone grey 'grid' No.56081 (opposite), without any body side freight sector decals, trundles downhill towards Drongan on the Killoch branch, 23rd May 1997, with a loaded MGR bound for Fiddlers Ferry power station.

'HEAs' : Having been loaded at Killoch, Class 56 No.56032 (below) waits for clearance to leave the branch at Annbank Junction, Mossblown, on 3rd July 1999 to join the Mauchline Jct. - Ayr line with 'HEAs' loaded for Shrewsbury.

The 56 will first have to run to Falkland Yard for a reversal before retracing its steps, proceeding south via the ex-Glasgow & South Western route via Dumfries to Carlisle, thence the WCML to Crewe.   **Max Fowler (3)**

Enterkine Viaduct : Also known as *Crawfordston*, this viaduct was erected in 1872 as part of the Ayr - Cumnock railway line and used to transport coal from various open cast mines, until loading at Killoch ceased. On 30th April, No.66551 (above) crosses the viaduct (River Ayr) with 6E74, 18.57 Killoch - Drax.

Greenburn : Following the cessation of coal flows from Killoch and Ravenstruther, the remaining opencast loading points are at Greenburn and New Cumnock. This image is included to show the extent of opencast mining at Greenburn, which will now see more use. DBS Class 66/0 No.66198 (below) is seen at Greenburn on 13th March with open cast mining operations taking place in the foreground. This train will form 6E92, the 14.58 Greenburn - Drax.   **Donald Cameron (2)**

Butterwell Coal

6Z20, 10:37 Chaddesden - Butterwell	empty 'JRA' box wagons	
6Z21, 17:40 Butterwell - Thoresby	loaded train	
6Z22, 07:22 Thoresby - York Holgate	empty 'JRA' box wagons	
6Z20, 13:02 York Holgate - Butterwell	empty 'JRA' box wagons	

This new flow sees a Class 56 (DCR) working north of Newcastle on the East Coast Main Line for the first time in over 10-years, taking coal from Butterwell opencast site to Thoresby for washing and blending. Thoresby Colliery, near Edwinstowe, has been producing coal for more than 80 years and most of its coal goes to Cottam and West Burton power stations.

The contract begins in March and is scheduled to operate for 18 weeks, and Class 56 No.56311 has the honour of working the first trains. No.56311 then moves south to work the Willesden - Calvert spoil trains and ex-Fastline liveried 'grid' No.56301 works light-engine from Washwood Heath, to take over the duties. The first loaded train runs on 5th March, hauled by Class 56 No.56311 and a rake of 15 'JRA' bogie box wagons, numbered:

70.6790.006-1	70.6790.031-2	70.6790.043-7	70.6790.096-5	70.6790.065-0
70.6790.094-0	70.6790.085-8	70.6790.033-8	70.6790.064-3	70.6790.082-5
70.6790.062-7	70.6790.059-3	70.6790.061-9	70.6790.049-4	70.6790.095-7

Week commencing 15th April sees the source of blending coal amended to take in Kellingley (east of Knottingley) with the train plan operating as set out below:

6Z22, 03:34 Thoresby - York Holgate	MFO	empty 'JRA' box wagons	
6Z22, 06:34 Thoresby - York Holgate	TWTHO	empty 'JRA' box wagons	
6Z22, 06:44 Thoresby - York Holgate	SO	empty 'JRA' box wagons	
6Z20, 13:02 York Holgate - Butterwell	TTHO	empty 'JRA' box wagons	
6Z20, 17:01 York Holgate - Kellingley	MWFO	loaded train	
6Z21, 17:40 Butterwell - Thoresby	TTHO	loaded train	
6Z21, 19:56 Kellingley - Thoresby	MWFO	loaded train	

Last 'Grid' Workings

Looking back through the records, it would appear that the last freight service to be 'booked' for Class 56 traction, *north of Newcastle'*, was the Alcan aluminium ingot traffic:

6V49, 14:53 Lynemouth - Newport ADJ   6N61, 05:44 Tees Yard - Lynemouth

---

(Selective Images) :

(Top Left) : After an extremely testing week, the photographer finally manages to shoot this new working. Following two car failures, an early morning sojourn for a third time down to Slade Hooton, the reward is the desired result - a 'grid' back at work on the South Yorkshire Joint Line. On 14th March, No.56311 passes the camera, with Laughton En Le Morthen church standing proud on the hillside, the 'grid' -heading north with the same train as the one depicted above; 6Z22, 07:00 Thoresby Colliery - York Holgate.

From Thoresby, 6Z22 reaches the ECML at Doncaster Decoy via;

- Clipstone East and West Junctions
- Shirebrook South and East Junctions
- Shireoaks West Junction
- Brancliffe East Junction
- 'South Yorkshire Joint Line'

(Bottom Left) : Ex-Fastline 'grid' No.56301 raises the echoes as it roars through Knottingley station on 2nd August 2013 during a thunderstorm with 6Z16, the 19:58 York Holgate - Kellingley Colliery loaded coal. The colliery, also known as the 'Big K', is a further three miles down the line.   **Mark Walker (2)**

Just like old times, a 'grid' returning to former stomping grounds. Here, on the ECML north of Newcastle, DCR No.56311 (above) passes Ulgham Lane on 12th March, slowing on the approach to Butterwell Junction with 6Z20, the 13:02 York Holgate - Butterwell - Butterwell and 'JRA' empties for loading with coal. Meanwhile, heading in the opposite direction, No.56301 (below) powers past Ulgham Lane Crossing with 6K61, the 17:40 Butterwell - Thoresby on 4th July, loaded today at Potland Burn. The view is almost 'continental', with internationally coded bogie box wagons forming the consist and the houses beside the main line decorated with terracotta roof tiles. **Martin Cook (2)**

6Z20

(Opposite) :

56301 (Top Right) is still in Fastline colours and passes Colton South Junction on 10th April with 6Z20, the 17:01 York Holgate - Kellingley, in readiness to load up with coal from the 'Big K' and then work 6Z21, the 19:56 Kellingley - Thoresby. This 'grid' was formerly No.56045.

The train is on the 'Up Normanton' line and is heading for Church Fenton; the road bridge visible in the background (top right of view) spans the East Coast Main Line.

56312 (Bottom Right) started life as No.56003. It is seen on 3rd April working 6Z20 and about to pass through Church Fenton with the empty 'JRAs' bound for Kellingley. In this view, the 56 is running on the 'Up Leeds' platform road, which it will leave at Church Fenton South Junction, in order to rejoin the 'up Normanton' line.

The itinerary for the southbound run of 6Z20 from York is:

York Holgate Sidings	(17:01hrs)	Colton Jct	(17:09)
Church Fenton	(17:15)	Milford Jct	(17:25)
Ferrybridge North Jct	(17:40)	Knottingley East Jct	(17:42)
Sudforth Lane Signal Box	(17:49)	Sudforth Lane Down GBRf	(17:51 - 18:11)
Kellingley Colliery	(18:12 - 19:57)		

Tom Robson (2)

(Top) :

56303 looks and sounds fantastic as it powers through Morpeth on 16th August, running today as 6Z15, the 08.38 Holgate Sidings - Potland Burn coal empties. These trains can be loaded at either Potland Burn or Butterwell, both very close to each other and accessed via the 'Blyth & Tyne' rail network. **Martin Cook**

Clay Sand

Background:

In June, the movement of 'clay sand' returns to rail after a gap of several years, operated by DB Schenker, hauled by a Class 59 or Class 66/0 loco, manned by Westbury crew.

The diagram is:

7Z26, 22:17	**Westbury - Burngullow**	empty 'MRL' box wagons
7Z27, 10:03	**Burngullow - Exeter Riverside**	loaded portion
0Z28, 15:48	**Exeter Riverside - Tavistock Junction**	light engine
7Z28, 18:32	**Tavistock Junction - Westbury**	loaded portion

The Product

By-products from the extraction of china clay (Kaolin) from decomposed granite consists of two main materials: 'Stent' (waste rock) and 'Tip Sand'. China Clay Tip Sand is defined as the washed material produced during the extraction of China Clay, comprising predominantly of quartz with some mica, which can be used in:

- Bitumen bound materials: a china clay sand asphalt base for Highway Works.

- Concrete

- Embankments: suitable for the construction of embankments and as bulk fill.

MendipRail Class 59/0 No.59001 'Yeoman Endeavour' (above) passes through Bodmin Parkway station on a very dull 24th June with 7Z27, the 11:13 Burngullow- Exeter Riverside loaded sand. This is believed to be the first Class 59/0-hauled freight in Cornwall.

Running along the north bank of the Teign estuary on 10th June, Class 66/0 No.66162 (above) hauls 7Z27, the 10:03 Burngullow - Exeter Riverside loaded sand past Bishopsteignton.

Meanwhile, another MendipRail Class 59/0, No.59005 'Kenneth J. Painter' (below), hauls an early running 7Z27, 11:13 Burngullow - Exeter Riverside along the banks of the River Teign, near Bishopsteignton, on Monday, 9th September. Due to unexpected problems with the loading equipment at Burngullow, this results in the train being sent back north empty! **Robert Sherwood (3)**

Lafarge and Buxton Cement Merger

During the first six months of 2013, there have been major changes to rail-bourne cement traffic flows as a result of the merger of Lafarge (Blue Circle) and Tarmac (Buxton cement). One of the conditions for approval of the merger was that the cement works at Hope had to be sold off to avoid a monopoly situation developing.

As a result, a major new player has come into being - Hope Construction Materials - the consequence being a change in cement flows, as described below:

CEMENT

Hope Construction

Earles Sidings - Dewsbury	6E91	Existing flow	FHH
Earles Sidings - Theale	6V94	Existing flow	FHH
Earles Sidings - Walsall	6Z65	**New flow**	DBS

Lafarge

Oxwellmains - Aberdeen	6A65	Existing flow	FHH
Oxwellmains - Inverness	6H51	Existing flow	FHH
Oxwellmains - Viewpark	6D62	Existing flow	FHH
Oxwellmains - Seaham	6E90	Existing flow	FHH
Oxwellmains - Carlisle	6M01	Existing flow	FHH
Oxwellmains - Leeds	6Z54	**New flow**	FHH
Tunstead - West Thurrock	6L89	**New flow**	FHH
Tunstead - Willesden	6A50	Existing flow	DBS
Tunstead - Westbury	6V82	**New flow**	FHH

AGGREGATE TRAFFIC

A spin off from this merger is that Tunstead Quarry is now seeing an increase in aggregate traffic with some exciting new flows and traction:

6E77, 11:49 Tunstead - Doncaster Decoy Yard	T/ThO	GBRf 66	**Box wagons**
6L77, 15:42 Tunstead - Peterborough Yard	WFO	GBRf 66	**Box wagons**
6V09, 14:14 Tunstead - Brentford	MWX	GBRf 66	**Bogie hoppers**
6Z93, 14:14 Tunstead - Brentford	WX	FHH 66	**Bogie hoppers**

(Opposite) : Tunstead Cement Flows

(Top Right) : FHH Class 66/6 No.66621 passes Milford with the new 6V82, Tunstead - Westbury loaded cement train, which is using the unique 'JGA' Bogie Cement Tank Hoppers. This is the first time these hoppers have been hauled by a FHH loco, usually only found on DBS cement flows from Tunstead to Leeds, Walsall and Willesden.

The train has just exited Milford Tunnel, which is on the Midland Main Line between Belper and Duffield in the Derwent Valley and runs under a hill called the 'Chevin'. The tunnel was built in 1840 by George and Robert Stephenson for the North Midland Railway and is 855 yards long.   **Ian Ball**

(Bottom Right) : "As the crow flies" .... well, not in this case, one is simply content to perch on a stanchion and observe FHH Class 70 No.70004 on 6L89, the 11:49 Tunstead - West Thurrock cement passing Bedford Midland station, platform 1, on 1st July. This is a fairly rare appearance for the class so far this spring / summer.   **Nigel Gibbs**

6V82 ▲   ▼ 6L89

6E28

There are many changes to cement and aggregate flows due to competition rules and one such example sees the Leeds cement being sourced from Oxwellmains (FHH) instead of Tunstead (DBS). Consequently, the last DBS cement flow to Leeds runs on 15th February using the unique 'JGA' Bogie 'Covhops. Class 66/0 No.66014 (above) is seen crossing the River Calder at Healey Mills, as 6M22, Leeds Hunslet - Tunstead cement empties skirts the now disused yard.

Derek Holmes

6V09 / 6Z96

A new flow of aggregate from Tunstead to Brentford runs on different days, using different railfreight operators and rolling stock. On 1st July, GBRf Class 66/7 No.66724 'Drax Power Station' (below) passes Edale signal box with the newly introduced 6V09, 14:14 Tunstead - Brentford, formed of a rake of FHH 'JGA' Bogie Aggregate Hoppers, nicknamed 'Jolly Green Giants'.

Alan Hazelden

Bardon Stone to Tinsley

Background

Aggregate Industries have created a new rail-served stone terminal at Tinsley, near Sheffield, and the first train runs on 6th June from Bardon Hill quarry.

Originally, planning permission was granted during 2012 and the site is adjacent to the Sheffield International rail terminal, consisting of a bottom discharge rail unloading shed, covered fine aggregates shed, ready mix concrete and asphalt plants, plus aggregate recycling facility.

Aggregate Industries are working alongside Amey PLC to deliver the 'Streets Ahead' highways maintenance for Sheffield City Council, whereby Amey have been awarded the maintenance and resurfacing contract for 25 years. This work will require a lot of stone, which will hopefully continue to be rail-borne.

Although the site of Tinsley Yard is a shadow of its former self, it is good to see new freight returning to the Sheffield area.

The Train

6Z48, 03:30 Bardon Hill - Tinsley

Consist

The train utilises 'Bardon' Bogie Aggregate Hoppers, coded 'JGA' and prefixed 'BHQ':

17111	17128	17101	17110	17121	17112	17116	17119	17108	17113	17129
17118	17123	17122	17104	17102	17125	17120	17114	17117	17115	17105

FHH Class 66/6 No.66607 (above) comes off the old Great Central route at Woodburn Junction on 6th June with the first working of the new Tinsley stone. This is 6Z49, the 11:19 Tinsley - Bardon Hill return empty stone working, which will now proceed via Sheffield Midland station, Chesterfield and Toton. This particular train has since been recoded 6M01. **Alan Padley**

Brentford Stone : GBRf Class 66/7 No.66706 'Nene Valley' (above) has arrived back at Tunstead with 6Z40 'JGA' stone empties, ready to be reloaded with a fresh payload to form 6V09 for Brentford. **Mick Tindall**

Westbury Cement : Running via the 'Marches' on 3rd June, No.66621 (below) approaches Sutton Bridge Junction, Shrewsbury, with 6M58, the 03:35 Westbury Lafarge - Tunstead empty cement tanks. **Mike Hemming**

Willesden Spoil

In April, the existing DBS flow from Willesden to the landfill site at Calvert switches to 'grid' traction, provided by DCR. The respective details are:

Old Flow:

6Z48, 08:50 Willesden E.T. -Calvert (loaded)   **6Z49, 18:26 Calvert - Willesden E.T.** (empties)

New DCR Flow: (Reporting details and timings)

6Z80, Willesden Euro Terminal - Calvert		6Z81, Calvert - Willesden Euro Terminal	
Willesden Euro Terminal	09:30 (depart)	Calvert	18:26 (depart)
Acton Main Line	10:13	Aylesbury	19:03
West Ruislip	10:38	Princes Risborough	19:19
Princes Risborough	11:12	West Ruislip	19:48
Aylesbury	11:29	Acton Main Line	20:10
Calvert	11:56 (arrive)	Willesden S.W.	20:17 - 21:40
		Willesden Euro terminal	22:00 (arrive)

The first train runs on 21st April with Class 56 No.56312 hauling 18 modified 'JRA' wagons from Chaddesden to Willesden via Loughborough & Peterborough in readiness for trains to commence running from Willesden.

Not what one would normally expect to see coming along the East Coast Main Line at Finsbury Park on Sunday, 21st April, ... DCR Class 56 No.56312 (above) passes through the station on the 'Up Fast' line with 6Z56, the 15:30 Chaddesden Sidings - Willesden ET. The 'grid' leaves the ECML at Copenhagen Junction and then goes via Camden Road to Willesden, ready to work 6Z80 the following day - yet another Class 56 hauled working to the landfill site at Calvert!   **Nigel Gibbs**

On the first day of DCR operation, No.56312 (above) passes Askett foot crossing on the Princes Risborough to Aylesbury branch with 6Z80, the 09:30 Willesden Euro Terminal - Calvert loaded spoil. Note the shiny round buffers!
David Stracey

Two 'grids' for the price of one and a rare sight indeed! No.56312 (below) has just arrived at Calvert on 24th April with 6Z80 and stands alongside the green DCR Class 56 No.56303, which is ready to leave with empty 'MBA' box wagons (6Z91) bound for Didcot power station.
Simon Howard

Felixstowe North Terminal Opens for Business

On 6th June, a new terminal at the country's largest container port opens, creating 1,500 new jobs and boasting the capability to handle the world's largest container ships. The expansion at the Port of Felixstowe is part of a £1bn investment drive.

The terminal consists of:

- **two berths**.

- **seven of the largest container cranes** in the world that will eventually cover the tracks. These are being built at the northern end of the Port of Felixstowe and will be shipped over from Ireland in sections, to be put together on site.

- **nine tracks** to receive freightliner and intermodal trains.

- a **'transverser'** has been installed for the first time at a container terminal, so that locos can easily be re-positioned onto clear tracks.

The Duke of York officially opened the new terminal at a special ceremony, accompanied by the CEO of Hutchinson Ports (UK) Limited, Clemence Cheng and the Department of Transport's maritime director, Ian Woodman.

The old 'North' terminal will now be known as 'Central' terminal, to avoid confusion.'

Selective Images:

(Left) : This panoramic view taken on 13th December 2012 shows the progress being made with the building of the new terminal at Felixstowe.

Most of the ground work has been done with regards to rail lines, just a case of resolving all the extra peripheral items, such as moving cranes into position, for example.

(Bottom Left) : As part of the official ceremony, ex-GWR 4575 Class 2-6-2 Prairie steam engine is brought in by road to provide an additional highlight for the event.

No.L150 is seen gently steaming atop some brightly coloured containers at the new terminal.

This steam engine, originally numbered 5521, was built at Swindon in 1927 and spent most of its working life on branch lines in the West Country.

In May 2013, at the request of London Underground, the engine is specially painted in red London Transport livery and numbered L150, commemorating the 150th anniversary of the Metropolitan Line.

The Traverser : FHH 'Powerhaul' Class 70 No.70001 (above) tests the new traverser

(Overleaf) : This was the spectators view of the opening ceremony and stage engineers pack away pyrotechnics and sound systems after the event. Smart looking DBS Class 66/0 No.66185 and GBRf Class 66/7 No/66709 'Sorrento' (Page 84) pose in some lovely summer sunshine. Meanwhile, No.70001 (Page 85), has uncoupled from its test train (4R98) and draws forward ready to go onto the traverser. It will then exit down line eight and couple back onto 4R98 and take it back to the old North terminal for working.

The Reception Sidings : A 'bird's eye' view of the sidings and No.66709 (below) stabled. **Michael Davies (6)**

Carlisle Departmentals switch 'TOC'

In August, after running for many years under the auspices of DBS, the Carlisle-based departmental workings switch to different traction providers:

DRS 6C02, 04:22 Crewe Basford Hall - Carlisle Yard 6K05, 12:18 Carlisle yard - Crewe B.H.

6C27, 09:42 Carlisle Virtual Quarry - Shap Quarry 6C28, 14:50 Shap Quarry - Carlisle V.Q.

GBRf 6M49, 08:08 Mossend - Carlisle Yard 6S51, 12:16 Carlisle Yard - Mossend

6C02 / 6K05 Timeline

The present day 6C02 and 6K05 started life in 2000, although there were spells beforehand when these 'trips' ran to & from Carnforth (Virtual Quarry ballast) and Workington steelworks (for rails), running under different reporting headcodes.

JULY 2000

6C02 : runs to & from Crewe Basford Hall instead of Bescot.

JULY 2002

6C02 : re-routed from WCML to the Settle & Carlisle.

MARCH 2005

6C02 : reverts back to WCML running, which is still the case today.

MARCH 2009

6K05 : re-routed via the Settle & Carlisle, although can still be sent via Shap.

This is an interesting train in terms of consist and can include a variety of 2-axle and bogie open box, hopper and flat wagons, which carry track hardware (crossovers, rails, sleepers, etc), plant machinery (cranes, diggers, tractors, etc) and materials (ballast, spoil, stone, etc)

This service could also have locos 'DIT' as a means of cost effective re-positioning moves.

6S51

GBRf break new ground on the WCML by venturing North of the Border, having taken over 6M49 / 6S51 departmental 'trips' from DBS. On an overcast 28th October, GBRf/Europorte Class 92 No.92038 'Voltaire' (above) approaches Bodsbury Crossing on the descent from Beattock Summit into the Upper Clyde Valley with 6S51, the 12:16 Carlisle Yard - Mossend. The consist is a mix of 2-Axle Low Sided Open Box Wagons and a single 'JNA' Bogie Ballast Wagon.   **Keith McGovern**

6C02 : Class 66/0 No.66127 (above) should make light work of the climb to Shap Summit, as it passes Greenholme at 06:39hrs on Saturday, 27th July, with the last 6C02 service operated by DBS. The consist on this inauspicious occasion is a single MPV, No.DR98952. **Ian Ball**

(overleaf) : 6K05 : DRS Class 66/4 No.66431 climbs through Smardale on 7th August with a very lengthy 6K05, 12:18 Carlisle Yard - Crewe Basford Hall formed mainly of 2-axle Wagons: 2 varieties of 'MHA' Low Sided Open Box Wagons and two varieties of 'MTA' Open Box Wagons. **Neil Harvey**

6C02 : Super power .... on 10th September, Malcolm-branded Class 66/4 No.66434 pilots fellow Class member No.66427 (below) on 6C02, 04:22 Crewe Basford Hall - Carlisle Yard with a consist of 4 x 5 vehicle sets of 'MRA' Bogie Side Tipping Ballast Wagons, in two variations of Network Rail livery. Only No.66434 will return south later with 6K05 to Crewe. **Kenny Marrs**

Colas Get a Slice of the Action too ....

The months of September and October see further Departmental changes in the southern part of the country with Colas Rail winning contracts from both DBS and Freightliner Heavy Haul, involving Eastleigh, Hoo Junction, Westbury and Whitemoor. The services are:

Westbury 'trips'

6Z28, 08:23 Westbury VQ - Newton Abbot

6Z30, 17:23 Westbury Yard - Eastleigh Yard

6M50, 07:36 Westbury VQ - Bescot VQ

6Z29, 12:39 Newton Abbot - Westbury VQ

6Z31, 20:47 Eastleigh Yard - Westbury Yard

6V46, 19:00 Bescot VQ - Westbury VQ

Hoo Junction 'trips'

6L37, 09:58 Hoo Junction - Whitemoor

7Y44, 04:22 Hoo Junction - Eastleigh

6Y42, 13:57 Hoo Junction - Eastleigh

6O36, 18:08 Whitemoor - Hoo Junction

6Y41, 09:04 Eastleigh Yard - Hoo Junction

7Y43, 19:57 Eastleigh Yard - Hoo Junction

(Selective Images) :

6Y42 : With lengthening shadows trying to encroach and spoil the view, this suggests that autumn is not far away. On 12th September, Class 66/8 No. 66850 'David Maidment OBE' (above) passes Worting Junction, Basingstoke, with 6Y42, the 13:57 Hoo Junction - Eastleigh Yard.

(previous page) : **6Z29** : On 2nd September, approaching seven o'clock in the evening, there's just about enough sunlight to record Class 47/7 No.47749 passing St. Denys with 6Z30, the 17:23 Westbury Yard - Eastleigh Yard. St. Denys is three miles north of Southampton city centre, opposite Bitterne Park on the River Itchen, and the area is named after the 12th century St. Denys Priory.   **Simon Howard (2)**

6Z29 : On 3rd September, No.47749 (top right) is out working again, but this time, returning to base with 6Z29, the 12:39 Newton Abbot Hackney Yard - Westbury Yard departmental, seen climbing Whiteball bank, near Burlescombe, formed of a 'YEA' Continuous Welded Rail Train.   **Peter Slater**

6M50 : Four days into Colas operation, No.66846 (bottom right) passes Uffington on 24 October with 6M50, 07:55 Westbury - Bescot. This is the site of Uffington loops, hence the wide track formation, and the redundant signals in the background. The loops were removed after the section from Challow to Wantage Road was quadrupled in the early 1990s.   **Martin Loader**

Background

The British Rail Class 47 is a diesel-electric loco developed in the 1960s by Brush Traction. A total of 512 Class 47s were built at Crewe Works and the Brush Falcon Works, Loughborough, between 1962 and 1968, which made them the most numerous class of British mainline diesel locomotive.

To mark more than 50 years of service, a special portfolio is included in this edition of *Loco Review* but, as there are so many locos, number series and livery variations, a sub-class has been chosen to feature ....

The Class 48s - a potted history

The British Rail Class 48 was a diesel loco class consisting of five examples, built at Brush Falcon Works, Loughborough, between September 1965 and July 1966. They were part of the British Rail Class 47 order, differing from their classmates by being fitted with a Sulzer V12 12LVA24 power unit producing 2,650 bhp .

The locos were numbered D1702 to D1706 and mainly worked out of Tinsley TMD, Sheffield, on passenger and freight work. In 1969, the majority moved to Norwich depot where they worked passenger expresses between there and London Liverpool Street.

As D1702 - D1706, all five initially carried the smart looking BR two-tone green livery followed by a coat of the monotone BR Blue livery, which became the norm in the early 1970s.

Conversion

The 12Lhe 12LVA24 engine proved unreliable and the locos spent more time out of service than their standard counterparts; engine failures were common.

Eventually, between 1968 and 1971, the 12LVA24 power units were removed and replaced with the standard 12LDA28 engine. D1702 was the first to be converted at Crewe Works, using parts from D1908, withdrawn after a serious accident, emerging in December 1969. All five locos had been converted by early 1971, becoming standard Class 47s, and the redundant power units were sold to SNCF and used in their Class 68000 loco.

In Service

The '48s' continued in service for many years afterwards, renumbered to 47114 - 47118, respectively, under the TOPS system. All were withdrawn from main line service during 1990 and 1991; the sole survivor, being No.47117 (D1705) which was bought for preservation by rail enthusiast and pop music producer, Pete Waterman.

Preservation

Only No.47117 survived the cutter's torch and is now owned by the Type 1 Locomotive Association and works on the Great Central Railway.

It has been restored to BR two-tone green livery with its pre-TOPS number D1705, but retaining its Class 47 engine.

It has also been named '*Sparrowhawk*' in the Brush Works tradition of naming locos after birds of prey (eg. 'Falcon', 'Kestrel').

(Opposite) :

47114 : For a time, in the post 'Speedlink' period between July 1994 and June 1997, Railfreight Distribution (RfD) concentrated its West Midlands European wagonload operations on Washwood Heath Yard rather than at Bescot. Having traversed the Sutton Park 'freight-only' line from Castle Bromwich, No.47114 (D1702) approaches Ryecroft Junction, Walsall, on 26th June 1995 with 6K63, the 12:55 (SX) Washwood Heath ' Longport 'Connectrail' service. Most of the train consist is made up of bogie tank wagons and 'PCA' type cement tanks destined for storage or the Marcroft wagon shops at Stoke-on-Trent. The service will avoid Bescot by way of the Pleck Junction to Darlaston Junction line.   **David J. Hayes**

47114

Sector Livery

When Trainload Freight was created in 1988, decals were applied to the body side of freight locos to denote which cargo sub-sector a loco was assigned to ....

Coal

Construction

'Speedlink' Distribution

General Use

Metals

Petroleum

..... No.47114 was the only one of the five locos to carry any such decals.

Construction : Class 47/0 No.47114 (above) starts away from Montrose station with the 17:15 Edinburgh Waverley - Aberdeen on the lovely sunny evening of 27th July 1989. At this time, the loco was allocated to Eastfield TMD, but still carried its Stratford 'Cockney Sparrow' depot plate and RailFreight blue & yellow square Construction livery decals. **Geoff Plumb**

'Speedlink' Distribution : RfD liveried No.47114 (below) is sporting red diamond decals, having just arrived at Stourbridge Junction with 6T50, the 09:05 (MWFO) Bescot - Brierley Hill European 'trip'. The consist includes several 'VAA' vans behind the loco as well as the usual high-capacity bogie Continental vans used for conveying imported steel. These European services were later marketed by RfD as Connectrail in March 1995, when much of this type of business began using the Channel Tunnel. **David J. Hayes**

47114

In Traffic	November 1965
Number	D1702
	47114 (March 1974)
Livery	(1) BR Two-Tone Green
	(2) BR Blue
	(3) BR Blue (grey/silver roof)
	(4) Railfreight Two-Tone Grey (Construction)
	(5) Railfreight Two-Tone Grey (Distribution)
	(6) Railfreight Two-Tone Grey (Unsectored)
	(7) Freightliner Two-Tone Green
Converted	July 1968 - December 1969

Allocation					
November 1965	41A	(Tinsley)	November 1970	40B	(Immingham)
May 1971	30A	(Stratford)	June 1989	ED	(Eastfield)
March 1992	TI	(Tinsley)	June 1996	CD	(Crewe)

Name	May 1997	*'Freightlinerbulk'*	(Named at Purfleet)
Withdrawn	October 1991		
Scrapped	March 2005	C. .F. Booth (Rotherham)	

(Above) : No.47114 undergoes maintenance at Tinsley 'Top Shed' on 4th April 1994.   **Nick Green**

Tinsley TMD opened during 1965 and was situated adjacent to, but at a higher level than the new Tinsley Marshalling Yard, alongside the Sheffield District Railway in Tinsley, near Sheffield. At one time or another, all five members of the Class 48 fleet had at least one spell allocated to Tinsley. During BR sectorisation, the depot came under the control of Railfreight Distribution (RFD) with responsibility for non-trainload freight operations. Unfortunately, the shed closed in 1998 and by June 2006 the site had been cleared.

(Overleaf) : Freightliner's unique green liveried No.47114 'Freightliner Bulk' (page 96) is approaching Wolvercote Junction on 18th May 1998 with 4S59, the 15:19 Millbrook - Coatbridge freightliner. Unfortunately, this stylish colour scheme was not perpetuated and all further Class 47 repaints received Freightliner grey livery, albeit using the same triangular logo as seen here.   **Martin Loader**

47115

In Traffic	September 1965					
Number	D1703					
	47115 (October 1973)					
Livery	(1) BR Two-Tone Green					
	(2) BR Blue					
	(3) BR Blue (grey/silver roof)					
Converted	February 1970 - November 1970					
Allocation	September 1965	41A	(Tinsley)	April 1969	32A	(Norwich)
	October 1969	30A	(Stratford)	February 1970	41A	(Tinsley)
	May 1971	30A	(Stratford)	May 1973	SF	(Stratford)
	September 1985	KD	(Kingmoor)	January 1987	CD	(Crewe)
	November 1987	TI	(Tinsley)	December 1988	IM	(Immingham)
Name	-					
Withdrawn	April 1991					
Scrapped	December 1995	M.R.J. Phillips (Frodingham)				

47115 : The tranquility surrounding the former Sutton Park station (closed January 1965), on the Walsall to Castle Bromwich 'freight-only' line, is momentarily disturbed on 11th May 1988 as No.47115 (above) passes with a lightweight 6V93, the 08:20 (SX) Mossend - Stoke Gifford 'Speedlink, formed of a delightful mix of tank wagons and vans. This service used to terminate at Severn Tunnel Junction Yard (closed 1987) and at one time travelled over the 'Welsh Marches' line via Shrewsbury and Hereford after leaving Crewe. To the left of the picture is the former General Post Office siding. **David J. Hayes**

(Previous Page) : White out conditions prevail at South Moreton on 9th February 1991. The horizon has disappeared and hedges and bushes in the distance merge with the sky as No.47115 kicks up the snow with 6E50, the 09:41 Langley - Lindsey petroleum empties. No.47115 was withdrawn exactly two months later and, after spending some time in store at Frodingham, was finally cut up in 1995. **Martin Loader**

47116

In Traffic	July 1966		
Number	D1704		
	47116 (January 1974)		
Livery	(1) BR Two-Tone Green		
	(2) BR Blue		
	(3) BR Blue (grey/silver roof)		
Converted	January 1971 - June 1971		

Allocation	July 1966	41A	(Tinsley)	June 1969	32A	(Norwich)
	October 1969	30A	(Stratford)	February 1970	41A	(Tinsley)
	January 1972	30A	(Stratford)	May 1973	SF	(Stratford)
	May 1989	TI	(Tinsley)	January 1990	BS	(Bescot)
	January 1990	CD	(Crewe)			
Name	November 1989	*'Gannet'*		Named unofficially at Tinsley		
Withdrawn	July 1990					
Scrapped	June 1994		C.F. Booth (Rotherham)			

47116 : Having arrived at Bescot behind a Class 85 electric loco, No.47116 (above) whisks 4O81, the 07:10 (SO) Coatbridge - Southampton Maritime Container Terminal freightliner through Hamstead station on 19th August 1989. This service will go via Coventry, Leamington Spa, Oxford, Didcot, Reading and Basingstoke to reach its Hampshire destination.   **David J. Hayes**

(Inset) : No.47116 passes through Cardiff Central station on 8th September 1989 with an unidentified 'Speedlink' service, which includes some empty 2-axle acid tanks bound for Hull Saltend. This train service would ultimately become 6E33, Baglan Bay - Hull Saltend.   **Simon Howard**

47117

In Traffic	November 1965			
Number	D1705			
	47117 (March 1974			
Livery	(1) BR Two-Tone Green	(2) BR Blue	(3) BR Blue (grey/silver roof)	
Converted	November 1970 - April 1971			
Allocation	November 1965	41A	(Tinsley)	June 1969	32A	(Norwich)
	October 1969	30A	(Stratford)	February 1970	41A	(Tinsley)
	May 1971	55A	(Holbeck)	October 1971	52A	(Gateshead)
	January 1972	34G	(Finsbury Park)	April 1972	30A	(Stratford)
	May 1973	SF	(Stratford)	November 1983	ED	(Eastfield)
	May 1986	HA	(Haymarket)	November 1986	ED	(Eastfield)
	January 1988	TI	(Tinsley)	January 1990	BS	(Bescot)
	January 1990	CD	(Crewe)			
	October 1990	TI	(Tinsley)			
Name	November 1989	'Sparrow Hawk'	Named unofficially at Tinsley	
Withdrawn	July 1991			
PRESERVED	December 1996 (Great Central Railway, Loughborough)			

(Opposite) : The only member of the Class 48 sub class to be preserved is No.47117 (ex-D1705) which is now proudly displayed in full working order at the Great Central Railway (GCR), Loughborough. The Great Central Railway is the UK's only double track, main line, heritage railway and is the only place in the world where full size steam engines can be seen passing each other!

At the GCR, No.47117 runs under the pre-TOPS number, D1705.

On 15th September 2007, No.D1705 'Sparrow Hawk' passes Woodthorpe on the Great Central Railway with a Loughborough - Leicester North service, looking superb in two-tone green livery.   **Nigel Gibbs**

47118

In Traffic	December 1965			
Number	D1706			
	47118 (October 1973)			
Livery	(1) BR Two-Tone Green			
(2) BR Blue				
	(3) BR Blue (grey/silver roof)			
	(4) BR Blue, Large Logo (grey roof)			
	(5) BR Blue, Large Logo (blue roof)			
Converted	March 1970 - November 1970			
Allocation	December 1965	41A	(Tinsley)	June 1969	32A	(Norwich)
	October 1969	30A	(Stratford)	February 1970	41A	(Tinsley)
	May 1971	55A	(Holbeck)	October 1971	40B	(Immingham)
	October 1972	52A	(Gateshead)	December 1972	30A	(Stratford)
	May 1973	SF	(Stratford)	May 1983	IS	(Inverness)
	July 1985	HA	(Haymarket)	November 1986	ED	(Eastfield)
	October 1987	CD	(Crewe)	May 1988	ED	(Eastfield)
	March 1989	TI	(Tinsley)			
Name	November 1989	'Lapwing'	Named unofficially at Tinsley	
Withdrawn	March 1991			
Scrapped	April 1995	M.R.J. Phillips (Doncaster)		

Settle & Carlisle Diversions : 47117 (above) is seen at Blea Moor with the diverted 12:10 Glasgow Central - Manchester Victoria on 11th March 1989, the passengers on board feeling decidedly chilly with a 'no heat' 47 at the front! Note the other Class 47 (No.47340) stabled beside the signal box in case anything failed.

Calder Valley 'Bins' : 47118 (below) starts after a signal check at Elland on 28th October 1987 with 6M62, the 12:08 Wakefield Cobra - Northenden empty 'Binliner'. Greater Manchester Council started dispatching household waste by train in 1981 from four transfer stations (Bredbury, Dean Lane, Northenden and Pendleton) offloading at a landfill site at Appley bridge, between Wigan and Southport. In 1987, train services were temporarily diverted to Wakefield.   **Neil Harvey (2)**

Departmental 'Trip' : 47117 (above), unofficially named 'Sparrow Hawk' by Tinsley TMD in November 1989, is illuminated in lovely evening light on 19th June 1990 as it comes off the Sutton Park line at Ryecroft Junction, Walsall, with a late running 9G10, 13:50 Northampton - Bescot Regional Civil Engineers' service.

'Speedlink' : 47118 (below) passes Stourbridge North Junction on 26th May 1989 and takes the Dudley line (now closed north of Round Oak) with 6M29, the 14:05 Taunton - Bescot. One of the main commodities conveyed by this service is Taunton Cider products, in high-capacity 'IZA' Cargowaggon twin-set vans and 'VGAs'. There is also a Freightliner portion (attached at Gloucester) loaded with containers from Bristol West, bound for Coatbridge. Stourbridge Junction station is visible in the background. **David J. Hayes (2)**

Headcodes - General Information

Before dealing with 'X' coded trains specifically, we first need to take a look at headcodes in general, to see how train reporting all fits together. The current format of train identification stems from 1960, at a time when all new diesel and electric locos built were fitted with a roller-blind display in a panel in the nose of the loco to show the full reporting number.

A train reporting number identifies a particular train service, which consists of:

- a single digit number, indicating the class (type) of train.

- a letter, indicating the destination area.

- a two-digit number, identifying the individual train.

Headcodes - Component Parts

Train Class

For operational reasons, certain trains are grouped into classes:

1	Express passenger train / postal / overhead line equipment train / snowplough
2	Ordinary passenger train.
3	Freight train running at more than 75 mph / railhead treatment train.
4	Freight train which can run up to 75 mph.
5	Empty coaching stock (ECS).
6	Freight train which can run up to 60 mph.
7	Freight train which can run up to 45 mph.
8	Freight train timed to run at 35 mph or less.
9	Class 373 train.
0	Light loco(s).

Destination letter

For long distance trains, the rail network is divided up into areas and each one is allocated a letter; very reminiscent of the old regions on British Rail:

E	Eastern	L	Midland	M	Midland
O	Southern	S	Scotland	V	Western

Other letters are used where the train remains within one region for its whole journey, for example 'G' for Birmingham and 'H' for Manchester.

Special Letters

In 2007, a special letter 'Q' was introduced for track recording trains, such as the Network Rail New Measurement Train. Trains with some specific requirements, such as *'out-of-gauge'* loads (see opposite) or the Royal Train, run with the letter 'X' and special trains (eg. railtours) have 'Z'.

Two-digit Identifier

As many trains are the same type, heading for similar destinations, the **last two digits** separate individual services or route.

Example : Train 6M81

This is a loaded steel service from Margam (Port Talbot) to Round Oak (West Midlands) and is limited to 60 mph, making it a class '6' train. It is going to the Midland region 'M' and is train number '81'. Similarly, locomotives on the way to pick up a train or running round to change the direction of travel are given the train number, but with a 0 prefix.

Out of Gauge - 'X' trains

Description

Basically, an **'X'** coded train refers to one which exceeds the height or width (or both!) of the UK loading gauge, so the train is restricted in terms of the lines along which it is permitted to travel. It may also be subject to specific speed restrictions at certain stations due to the danger of fouling canopies / platform edges. The load being carried may also attract this code.

Train documentation is issued on a 'train by train' basis, as the degree of overheight / width affects the restrictions which apply in each case.

Examples of trains which run with an **'X'** code are:

- car trains using double deck, open wagons.
- EMU 'drags' (such as Class 20-hauled LUL moves)
- trains conveying the Network Rail point and crossing carriers.
- pipe trains conveying large diameter pipes.
- dangerous loads.

Interestingly, the former 'White Rose' service from London King's Cross to Leeds, which utilised a Eurostar set, ran with a prefix of 1**X** due to the train's unusually long length.

Portfolio

While it is not always possible to give the details why a particular train is allocated an 'X' code, it is possible to provide you with a selection of images to illustrate 'X' rated trains!

Large Pipes

This image illustrates how large pipes overhang the bogie bolster wagons ('BDA' / 'BEA') which carry the pipes, making the train 'out of gauge'. So, an additional wagon is placed in between each pipe carrying wagon, usually a 2-axle 'RRA' runner, to accommodate any overhanging, The train in question here is 6X88, Hartlepool - Georgemas Junction, passing Murthly on the Highland Line.   **Jim Ramsay**

Pipe Trains

For comparison purposes, two images have been selected from the archives to illustrate the carriage of normal size pipes, which operate to WTT timetable reporting.

These trains ran from Stanton Gate (near Toton) to Tees Dock (for export) and from Hartlepool to Aberdeen (for North Sea oil industry).

Both of these services used conventional wagons, so no 'runners' were needed, as there is no overhanging .

6N77 : Prior to its transition to a DBS 'super tug' in 2012, the ex-Loadhaul black & orange livery Class 60 No.60059 'Swinden Dalesman' (above) is seen on 28th July 2006 hauling a short rake of small pipes bound for Raithes Farm (Aberdeen) via Mossend. Some pipes did go to Leith (Edinburgh) beforehand, for coating.

The train is the early running 6N77, 21:00 Hartlepool - Tees Yard which is passing Cowpen Bewly at 18:34hrs on the main line between Seaton Carew and Billingham. The pipes will go forward to Scotland overnight, via Mossend.

     Wagons : 'BTA' Bogie Bolster Pipe Wagons

6Z71 : Class 66/0 No.66145 (below) passes Colton South Junction on 23rd August 2005 with 6Z71, the 08:07 Stanton Gate - Tees Dock, carrying pipes for export.

     Wagons : 'BDA' / 'BEA' Bogie Bolster wagons   'SEA' 2-axle Open Plate Wagons

Ian Ball (2)

Georgemas Junction Pipes

6X88

DBS Class 66/0 No.66101 (above) passes Inveresk, Musselburgh, on 11th October 2011 working 6X88, the 05:38 Hartlepool - Georgemas Junction pipe train, which has 2-axle 'RRA' runners inserted in the consist to cater for the overhanging pipes.   **Keith McGovern**

(Overleaf) : : On 18th September 2012, Class 66/0 No.66104 crosses the Royal Border Bridge with 6X88 and enters Berwick-upon-Tweed station with pipes for the North Sea gas & oil industry; 'RRAs' are only needed for the larger pipes, which are at the rear of the train.   **Kenny Marrs**

6E69 : Returning from Georgemas Junction, the empty pipe carriers can run as a WTT service, as it is now 'in gauge'. On 8th November 2012, No.66101 (below) passes Newcraighall with the bogie bolsters and 'RRAs' in tow, running as 6E69, the 17:45 (ThO) Georgemas Junction - Hartlepool.   **Keith McGovern**

Car Carriers

6X44 : Work stained No.66170 (above) passes South Moreton on 7th May 2013 with 6X44, the 14:38 Dagenham Dock - Didcot, conveying Ford vans and cars. This location is reasonably clear until later in the year, when the foreground vegetation starts to get in the way.   **Martin Loader**

(Previous Page) : **6X38** : A nice 'mixed freight" - No.66097 hauls 6X38, Eastleigh - Didcot through Purley on Thames, which would normally run as 6V38, Marchwood - Didcot. However, 6V38 terminated at Eastleigh and 6X38 created in order to convey Ford cars and vans from the docks at Southampton.   **Guy Houston**

6X44 : Another view of this train, this time with No.66067 (below) passing Cholsey Manor Farm on the Great Western Main Line, bound for staging at Didcot, before going forward to Mossend as 6X65.   **Ian Ball**

Wagonload

6X02 : Class 66/0 No.66161 (above) passes Colton Junction on 10th July 2007 heading north with 6X02, Didcot - Redmire, consisting a solitary 'VGA' van plus 'KFA' (Warflat) and 'KWA' (Warwell) bogie vehicle transporters, used to convey army vehicles on behalf of the MoD (Ministry of Defence).

6X12 : On 3rd April 2009, Class 92 No.92015 'D H Lawrence' (below) climbs to Shap Summit at Little Strickland with 6X12, Carlisle Yard - Eastleigh 'Enterprise' which has MoD containers sandwiched between two 'OCA' 2-axle wagons - the question is, what's inside the containers, munitions, perhaps?   **Ian Ball (2)**

6X65 : Class 60 No.60054 (above) is a rare visitor to Scotland after being commandeered to work 6X52, Portbury - Mossend from Carlisle, retimed and given a new headcode. The train length is a staggering 2,182ft and it has to run non-stop all the way to Mossend, holding up a number of West Coast passenger trains, as the passing loops are too small. No.60054 and No.92037 'Spirit of Dagenham' are passing Ravenstruther on 3rd August 2012 with 6X65, Carlisle - Mossend. **Guy Houston**

5X47 : 'Dead Hauled Transit' is the terminology to describe a unit move like the one illustrated here. Autumn is drawing to an end, but the leaves on the trees are still displaying some brilliant red and golden brown colours and, on 17th November 2012, GBRf Class 66/7 No.66710 'Phil Packer BRIT' tows EMUs No.466015 + No.466009 near Dartford with 5X47, Tonbridge Yard - Slade Green EMU Depot.   **Ian Cuthbertson**

Rolling Stock Moves

6X39 : Colas Rail had the honour of hauling new Virgin West Coast Pendolino sets and coaches to Longsight and Edge Hill from July 2011. These had come via the Tunnel from Alstom's plant in Savigliano, Italy, following closure of their Washwood Heath works. Each train ran 'Out of Gauge' as 6X39.

On 31st May 2012, Class 66/8 No.66848 (left) plus some 'Pendo' coaches has emerged from Eynsford Tunnel (828 yards long) and passes under the M25 Motorway near Swanley working 6X39, the 05:35 Dollands Moor - Longsight CMD.

Ian Cuthbertson

8X23 : Running over an hour late, GBRf Class 66/7 No.66731 (below) passes Stenson Junction with 8X23, the 09:30 Derby Litchurch Lane - Old Dalby, a move to take a new London Underground 'S Stock' unit (No.1001) for testing.

The additional wagons are there to provide the necessary brake force. A number of these trains have been running recently, most hauled by Class 20s, as new units built at Derby are delivered to Neasden depot after testing. **Martin Loader**

5X70 : EWS liveried Class 67 No.67021 (above) passes Brondesbury on the North London Line leading 5X70, the 10:00 Gillingham EMUD - Doncaster West Yard, a move taking Class 508 No.508210 to Doncaster for overhaul. The ensemble is passing the camera in the region of 10 minutes ahead of schedule. **James Welham**

7X80 : DBS Class 92 No.92026 'Britten' (below) tows two new Class 380 EMUs, No.380107 + No.380109, on 17th September 2010, sandwiched between some international 'Cargowaggons'. The train is 7X80, Dollands Moor - Polmadie and is near Chislehurst in Kent.

The Class 380 'Desiro' is a electric multiple unit operating on the Ayrshire Coast Line and Inverclyde Line in Scotland. The construction was awarded to Siemens and announced by Transport Scotland in 11 July 2008 with 38 sets ordered, comprising 22 three-car and 16 four-car units.   **Ian Cuthbertson**

Network Rail 60ft 'IFA' Twin Bogie Tilt-Bed Point & Crossing Carriers

Network Rail has a fleet of 26 tilting wagons, built by Kirow (Germany) which can tilt their loads so that pre-constructed panels of track, which are normally too wide to be carried by rail, can be transported directly to site. When the wagons arrive, the decks are moved back to a horizontal position for the panels to be unloaded and slotted quickly into place.

The track panels used to replace points have a sleeper length of up to 3.7 metres, which is too long to fit within the network's '**W6a gauge**'. The wagon deck can tilt up to an angle of approximately 60 degrees, enabling the panels to fit within the width of the railway.

The wagon deck is 22.5m long, sufficient for the majority of switches and crossings but, for longer panels, the deck can be extended to allow panels of up to 26.5m to be carried. Due to the gauge constraints, these wagons must be moved under a '**X**' reporting code.

(Above) : Close up of 'IFA' wagon No.35.70.9378.012-2 at Whittlesea.　　　**Richard A Jones**

(Below) : **6X06** : FHH Class 66/5 No.66531 speeds north at Raskelf on the ECML with 6X06, Doncaster Decoy - Wooden Gate Jct. engineer's train, which includes 'IFAs' in the consist.　**Ian Ball**

Infrastructure

6X01 : This WTT service (the 10:17 Scunthorpe - Eastleigh) of welded rail is seen between Radley and Culham hauled by 66107 (top right) on 30th April.

It is coded 'X' due to the length of the rails, protecting them from too much 'bending', by having the train routed to avoid sections of lines with severe curvature.

6X30 : GBRf Class 73s No.73212 + No.73213 (middle) pass Northfleet double-heading 6X30, Kentish Town - Hoo Junction welded rail train. The reinstated trackwork deviating to the left is used for 'Crossrail' spoil trains.   **Ian Cuthbertson (2)**

6X05 : This is actually 6K05, the 12:18 Carlisle Yard - Crewe Basford Hall, but running under 'out of gauge' restrictions due to some 'IFAs' in the consist.

This service could also be used as a way of moving locos and on 9th January 2012, Class 66/0 No.66172 (below) passes Waitby on the Settle & Carlisle with two other 'sheds' (Nos.66161 and 66102) 'DIT'.
                    Ian Ball

Light Engine Movements were once restricted to 5 locos coupled up, but current practice now allows a maximum of 10-locos to run in convoy, albeit to out-of-gauge ('X') reporting restrictions. On 31st August, a convoy of five 'sheds' - Nos.66093 + 66034 + 66186 + 66230 + 66132 + 66134 (above) head up Shap at Scout Green, running as 0X19, Warrington Arpley - Carlisle.

Keith McGovern

Extensive engineering work on the Southern Region, plus 'Crossrail' and 'Thameslink' projects, necessitate a large number of GBRf locos and, instead of returning locos individually to their home base, they usually move together for operating and financial efficiency. Here, 0X66, Tonbridge - Eastleigh, formed of 6 x '73s' and a '66' (Nos.73213 + 73208 + 66743 + 73205 + 73206 + 73119 + 73212) (below) are seen leaving Sevenoaks Tunnel on 30th July 2012.

Alan Hazelden

On 19th April, Class 20s No.20227 and No.20189 (above) are seen in their new liveries while stabled at Didcot during their trip (0Z20) from Butterley to West Ruislip. No.20227, the former Haymarket loco, is in London transport colours of grey livery with wrap-round red cab ends and a blue sole bar.   **Simon Howard**

A trio of 'choppers' .... Nos.20142 + 20189 + 20227 (opposite) head through West Brompton on 7th May with 0Z20, this time running from West Ruislip LUL to Clapham Yard. The train was due to pick up VEP unit No.3417 at Clapham Junction and continue to the Swanage Railway for their diesel gala. In the event, problems with the unit meant the Class 20s later continued their journey on their own.   **Stuart Chapman**

Close up of No.20189 (below) at Didcot in London Transport Metropolitan red livery.   **Simon Howard**

Background

During the past few years, more and more locos are receiving a face lift into new colours to brighten up the rail scene and there does not seem to be any abatement, as this portfolio will demonstrate. Here's what's been happening since the last edition of *'Loco Review'* ....

Class 20

Nos.20189 and 20227 have been repainted into London Transport colours to celebrate the 150th anniversary of the London Underground, the Metropolitan Line in particular. Known as the 'Tube', London Underground was the first metro system in the world, the original Metropolitan Railway opening in 1863 between Paddington and Farringdon.

Class 66 (DBS)

The original 'shed' No.66001 receives a new coat of paint of DB Schenker corporate red, fittingly so, as it is the Class's 15th anniversary year - 1998 marking the start of the 'GM Revolution'.

The General Motors-built No.66001, the first new loco to be ordered by English, Scottish and Welsh Railways (EWS), arrived at Immingham Docks on 18th April 1998, one of 250 locos in a £500-million investment programme in new locos and rolling stock. The loco had been transported across the Atlantic Ocean from Albany, New York, in the hold of Dutch-registered MV 'Fairload.'

Class 66 (Freightliner)

"First Class 66 in Powerhaul livery"

Class 66/5 No.66504, one of Freightliner's intermodal Pool, becomes the first Class 66 to be outshopped in Powerhaul colours. Having entered LNWR Crewe in early March, the loco returns to traffic in early May and joins other Class 66 locos so applied in Powerhaul colours, albeit those working in Poland and Australia, and smart the new look is too!

66001 : Fresh from the paint shop! Complete with silver buffer embellishments, DBS Class 66 No.66001 (above) passes Uffington (between Stamford and Peterborough) on 2nd April leading 6L41, the 09:25 Mountsorrel - Barham loaded aggregate service. Having left Mountsorrel some 44 minutes late, the gleaming 'shed' is now only 24 minutes early, after avoiding the booked stop at Oakham. The day's train consists of 22 'PGA' and 2 'JGA' wagons, weighing in at 1,199 tonnes.
                                                                                                            James Welham

66504 (below) sweeps round the curve at Cargo Fleet, approaching Middlesbrough, at the head of a sparsely loaded 4D07, the 14:29 (TWThO) Wilton - Leeds freightliner. Although the growth of lineside trees is doing its best to mask the background, you can still just about see one of the gas holders at Redcar steelworks, plus the adjacent Lackenby steel plant.
                                                                                                            Ian Ball

66504 : Freightliner take the opportunity to start repainting their Class 66 fleet into 'Powerhaul' colours and the first such example is Class 66/5 No.66504. On 11th May, No.66504 (above) is seen at Millbrook on what is believed to be one of the loco's first outings in the new colours, working 4B08, Southampton Maritime FLT - Millbrook. This 'trip' is to move empty flats for storage over the weekend.   **Simon Howard**

66001 (below) is approaching Waterbeach on 5th April, and near journey's end, looking impressive at the head of 6L62, the 14:48 Mountsorrel - Chesterton Junction loaded self discharge train. A set formation usually consists of four varieties of 'PHA' 2-axle wagons, coded 'PHA' - P / Q / R and S, plus a 'KJA' Self Discharge Bogie Unloading Wagon.   **Alan Hazelden**

"CABLE THIEVES: WE'RE WATCHING YOU"

No.57307   Chelmscote   1st May   **Nigel Gibbs**

Recently acquired by DRS, Class 57 No.57307 'Lady Penelope' has been specially adorned with an eye catching message.

Supported by Network Rail and the British Transport Police, this new marketing initiative is aimed at targeting thieves who steal signalling cable, which causes huge disruption and cost. Perhaps, the sight of this ex-'Thunderbird' will put thieves off contemplating cable theft!

Foreign Interlopers

No.664025 (66750)   Dollands Moor   11th June   **Michael Wright**

'RUSH RAIL'

Newly imported GBRf Class 66, No.664025 (which will become No.66750) arrives in June from Germany and No.66701 is sent to pick it up and take it to Peterborough.

No.66750 carries Beacon Rail blue base livery, that of a German firm, but has Swedish branding for 'Rush Rail'.

However, this loco never worked for the firm, or in Sweden in the end, and is the only loco to carry this livery too!

'TURKISH DELIGHT'

Built in 2011 as a demonstrator for Turkish Railways, Class 70 No.70099 is transferred to the UK in 2012.

It carries its original all-over green livery, but without yellow warning panels, which will need to be added to enable it to run on the national network. It will then be re-numbered 70801.

The loco could see use by either Colas Rail (timber) or GBRf (coal / intermodal) and, if successful, could lead to a potential fleet order.

No.70099   Crewe, Basford Hall   1st June   **Jim Ramsay**

Class 66 (GBRf)   **"Dutch Imports"**

Three recently purchased Class 66 locos from Holland make their way from Dollands Moor to the Midlands Railway Centre at Butterley on 21st December 2012, hauled by Class 66/7 No.66735, where they will be made ready for use on our rail system.

The locos, after being built in the USA, were shipped to Holland and stored at Rossendaal. At the time of going to press with this book, the three loos are still in all-over grey livery and are numbered:

| 66747 | 66748 | 66749 |

The ex-Dutch Class 66s acquired by GBRf look impressive in grey livery, which will no doubt turn to a shade of blue at some stage in the future. Here, No.66749 (above) is seen heading along the ECML at Copmanthorpe Crossing, just north of Colton Junction, on 27th August with 6H30, the 09:45 Tyne Dock - Drax power station loaded biomass hoppers. Note the small number (66749)3260 on the front.   **Fred**

GBRF's new trio of Dutch Class 66s (Nos:66747, 66748 and 66749) are seen getting a tow from GBRf Class 66/7 No.66735 (above) as they pass Tudeley, just outside Tonbridge on the Paddock Wood side. The train is running as 0L66, the 09:30 Dollands Moor - Butterley.   **Alan Hazelden**

Meanwhile, after being 'kitted out' to run on our rail network, GBRf's ex-Dutch Class 66/7 No.66748 (below) is pressed into service on 19th August and is seen passing Seaton Carew with 6H30, the 09:45 Tyne Dock - Drax loaded biomass. Seaton Carew station is visible in the distance.   **Martin Cook**

'Dutch Imports' is reminiscent of the late '80s and early '90s, when some locos were in departmental use and painted in grey livery, prior to the application of a smart-looking civil engineer's 'Dutch' livery of yellow and grey.

(Top Right)	: 33201
	Eastleigh, 1989
Built	: BRCW, Smethwick
In Traffic	: 1962 as D6586
Allocated	: Hither Green
Preserved	: Midland Railway, Butterley
(Middle)	: 37054
	Thornaby, 1990
Built	: EE Vulcan Foundry
In Traffic	: 1962 as D6754
Allocated	: Darnall
Scrapped	: Motherwell September 2003
(Below)	: 47333 **'Civil Link'**
	Bescot, 1990
Built	: Brush Falcon Works
In Traffic	: 1965 as D1814
Allocated	: D16 Division
Scrapped	: C.F.Booth, Rotherham June 1998

Ian Cuthbertson Collection (3)

Steam

"Blue is the Colour, ..."

not for Chelsea Football Club, but two great steam locomotives:

A1 4-6-2 'Peppercorn' Pacific, No.60163 'Tornado'

In September 2012, at the A1 Trust's annual convention, it was announced that *'Tornado'* would be repainted into British Railway's Express **Passenger Blue** livery.

The blue is based on Caledonian blue, the livery of the Caledonian Railway, which was only applied to Express locos (like the A1s) for a few years before repainting into Brunswick green.

Tornado gets its repaint at Southall into BR Express Passenger Blue and is unveiled at Didcot Railway Centre on 24 November 2012.

This latest livery means 'Tornado' will now have sported all 4 liveries carried over the life of some of the earlier A1 locos. ie:

- 'Tornado' first appeared in 2008 and undertook her test runs in **grey undercoat**, described as 'works grey' in a 'satin finish'.

- Her first full livery is LNER-style express passenger **apple green**.

- In late 2010 / early 2011, while undergoing winter maintenance at the NRM (York), 'Tornado' is repainted into her second full livery, British Railway's **Brunswick green**.

4-6-0 GWR 'King' Class No.6023 'King Edward II'

After an extensive period undergoing overhaul, No.6023 re-entered service on the Mid-Norfolk Railway on 4 June 2011, as part of a running-in programme leading to a return to the main line. On 6 September 2012, she is moved to Loughborough (Great Central Railway) for firebox repairs and some other minor repairs.

'King Edward II' finally **makes her debut for fare-paying passengers** on the Great Central Railway during the weekend of 26th / 27th January 2013 and no one is disappointed with the outcome!

(Overleaf)

Selective Images

PROFILE of a 'KING'

No.6023 'King Edward II' in action on the Great Central Railway

The Great Central Winter Gala has a special guest star in January - the debut of GWR King Class 4-6-0 No 6023 'King Edward II' on the award winning Leicestershire heritage line. Fresh from overhaul the loco, in vibrant blue livery, has its first outing for fare-paying passengers.

The 'King' also features during a 'Vintage Easter Festival' to celebrate all things steam from Friday, 29th March to Monday, 1st April. The GCR run a busy timetable over these and several other weekends and here is a small selection of images featuring 'King Edward II' back at work. The GCR runs for 8-miles linking Leicester North - Rothley - Quorn & Woodhouse - Loughborough.

(Top Left) : **Swithland Sidings** : The 'King' puts on a good show passing through Swithland sidings, where the single line to Mountsorrel deviates from the main running lines.

(Bottom Left) : **Loughborough** : No.6023 leaves Loughborough, flanked by two impressive semaphore signals.

(Above) : **Swithland Sidings** : The 'King' is viewed from the other side of the line passing the re-erected signalbox and fully operational semaphore signals.   **Alan Padley (3)**

(Below) : **Quorn & Woodhouse** : No.6023 King Edward II making its debut on the Great Central Railway on 25th January, working 2A06, the 10:00 Loughborough - Leicester North.   **Mark Walker**

In August 2007 GBRf name, what will ultimately be four locos, a member of their Class 66/7 fleet after a famous English football club - this being No.**66725** 'Sunderland'.

All the nameplates are replicated after those carried by the former LNER B17 'Sandringham' or 'Footballer' Class of 4-6-0 steam loco, built between 1948 and 1955 (see below). The only exception is Class 66/7 No.66736, which is named 'Wolverhampton Wanderers', even though no B17 steam loco actually carried this name.

'B17' Profile

LNER No.	BR No.	Name	Built	Rebuilt	Withdrawn
2851	61651	Derby County	March 1936	June 1953	August 1959
2854	61654	Sunderland	April 1936	April 1948	November 1959
2861	61661	Sheffield Wednesday	June 1936	August 1955	July 1959

The football on each of the diesel loco's nameplate is flat due to loading gauge restrictions.

66725

GBRf 'Barbie' liveried Class 66 No.66725 'Sunderland'(above) is pictured on 30th November 2012 rattling towards a frosty Bainton (between Stamford to Peterborough) leading 6L76, the 07:05 Stud Farm - Whitemoor loaded ballast service, which consists of 20 'IOA' ballast boxes. Signalling problems in the Hinckley area mean the train is running around an hour behind schedule.

It's 10 years since GBRf named one of their Class 66/7 locos - on 11th November 2003, No.66715 is named 'Valour', at a special service to honour the dead of two world wars. In a simple but poignant ceremony at the site of Sheffield's former Victoria station, GBRf General Manager, Ward Simpson, unveiled No.66715 in front of invited guests, including the Very Reverend Peter Bradley, Dean of Sheffield. Earlier, the Dean had rededicated a newly restored First World War memorial to the memory of 1304 employees of The Great Central Railway Company.

The original 'Valour' was a Great Central Railway Class 9P (LNER B3) 4-6-0 steam loco, No.1165, named in honour of those who died in the First World War, entering service in 1920.   **James Welham**

66725 'Sunderland'

Mr Niall Quinn, chairman of Sunderland Football Club, names No.66725 on Friday, 10th August 2007 at the Port of Tyne; several former 'Black Cats' stars, including Jim Montgomery and Bobby Kerr, join Niall and over 100 guests at the event.

The last loco to carry this name was B1 No.61654, which took the victorious 1937 Sunderland team to Wembley for the cup final against Preston North End.

'Sunderland'   Ian Cuthbertson

66726 'Sheffield Wednesday'

On 11th September 2009 at Sheffield Midland station, No.66726 is named 'Sheffield Wednesday' in an event sponsored by wagon builder W H Davis.

Recently retired Chairman from W H Davis, Mr Derrick Sharpe, hands over a replica nameplate to the 'Wednesday' chairman, Mr Lee Stafford.

No.66726 works a special train (2Z30) from Sheffield to Manchester and back, 'The Wednesday Limited'.

'Sheffield Wednesday'   Ian Cuthbertson

66729 'Derby County'

First GBRf name No.66729 'Derby County' on 16th April 2010, to commemorate their contract with Bombardier Transportation, to deliver new underground stock.

Nigel Clough, Derby County manager said: "This is a great gesture and something we are all delighted about. The rail industry is extremely important to Derby and has always had a big impact on Derby County itself. It will be a proud moment to see a loco emblazoned with our name on it".

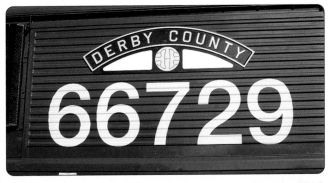

'Derby County'   Courtesy GBRf

66736
'Wolverhampton Wanderers'

This is the fourth and final '66/7' loco to be named. The naming of No.66736 takes place on 2nd December 2011, at a special unveiling ceremony held at Wolverhampton station.

The naming is thanks to a campaign by teenage Wolves fan Harry Cartwright. Harry tirelessly campaigned for the naming and attracted support from celebrity Wolves fans including the lead singer of Led Zeppelin, Robert Plant.

'Wolverhampton Wanderers'   Courtesy GBRf

66729

No.66729 (above) poses for the camera at GBRf's Peterborough base prior to the official naming, resplendent in First Group livery of indigo blue with pink and white stripes. **Courtesy GBRf**

The loco is now in GB Railfreight / Europorte colours of corporate blue with orange cab ends and orange stripes. After a grey start, it's clear blue skies on the afternoon of 15th November 2011, as No.66729 (below) rattles towards Tufts No.2 crossing in the outskirts of March, leading 4E33, the 11:20 Felixstowe South - Doncaster Railport intermodal. **James Welham**

66726

Amidst the red sandstone cliffs, No.66726 (above) hauls 6V55, the 22:05 Aldwarke - Exeter Alphington Road (via Newton Abbot) empty scrap wagons along the sea wall at Dawlish on Saturday, 18th May 2013. The consist is a rake of 'JXA' Bogie Scrap Wagons. **Robert Sherwood**

66736

Meanwhile, No.66736 (below) heads past Addison, near Blaydon on the Tyne Valley line, with 6Z58, the 11:00 (MWO) Hardendale - Lackenby limestone on 15th April, formed of eight 'JIA' Polybulk wagons. **Martin Cook**

'60' Numbers on the Rise

DBS start 2013 with a fleet of 21 Class 60s - **16** actually in traffic - the highest number for several years, thanks to the 'Super 60' overhaul schedule, instigated in January 2012. The Company has sufficient Class 60s to handle the heavier freight trains, bringing to an end any further possibility of trialling Class 59/2s and 2 x Class 66/0s on such trains.

Class 60 fleet - 06:00hrs, Wednesday, 2nd January 2013

Number	Pool	Location	Allocation
60007	WCBK	Immingham	6V70, Lindsey - Colnbrook
60010	WFMU	Toton	
60011	WCAI	Westerleigh	6E41, Westerleigh - Lindsey
60015	WCBI	Kingsbury	6E54, Kingsbury - Humber
60017	WCBI	Scunthorpe	6V66, Scunthorpe - Llanwern
60019	WCAI	Warrington	Liverpool BKTM - Fiddlers Ferry coal circuit
60020	WFMU	Toton	
60024	WSSK	Toton	
60040	WFMU	Toton	
60045	WCAK	Hinksey yard	(Super Shunter)
60049	WCAK	Eastleigh yard	
60054	WFMU	Toton	
60059	WCBK	Oakleigh	6H03, Oakleigh - Tunstead
60063	WCAI	Jarrow	6D43, Jarrow - Lindsey
60065	WCAI	Robeston	6B13, Robeston - Westerleigh
60071	WCBK	Peak Forest	6J46, Peak Forest - Hope Street
60074	WCAI	Warrington	Liverpool BKTM - Fiddlers Ferry coal circuit
60079	WCAI	Theale	6B33, Theale - Robeston
60091	WCBI	Tees yard	
60092	WCBI	Rotherham Steel Term.	6D94, Rotherham - Hull
60099	WCAI	Warrington	6F16, Fiddlers Ferry - Liverpool BKTM

'Booked' Duties

Petroleum :   Lindsey refinery - Colnbrook (6V70) / Jarrow (6N03) / Westerleigh (6V98)
Robeston refinery - Westerleigh (6B13) / Theale (6A11)

Limestone : Peak Forest - Hope Street (6J46)   Tunstead - Oakleigh (6F05)

Coal   : Liverpool BKTM - Fiddlers Ferry p.s. (6F74, 6F77, 6F81, 6F84, 6F85, 6F89)

Portfolio

In this particular issue of *Loco Review*, we take a look at new 'tugs' reinstated to traffic since January 2013, plus 'tugs' at work on duties other than the 'booked' duties described above.

60062
'Stainless Pioneer'

Nameplate (left) bestowed on No.60062 to commemorate the Centenary of stainless steel production in Sheffield. The name is dedicated at a special event at Tinsley on 13th June.

Craig Adamson

Departmental 'trips'

60071 *'Ribblehead Viaduct'* (above) has been on "supershunter" duties at Eastleigh, but is occasionally let out to play at weekends. Amazingly for Kent-based photographers, on 17th February it is allocated to work 6N01, Eastleigh - Hoo, which is seen here at Tovil crossing, near Maidstone.   **Alan Hazelden**

(Overleaf)

60020 (Page 138, top) idles away the hours of darkness in the yard at Whitemoor on 4th February, having earlier worked in from Toton, following a light engine move (0F54) from Peak Forest.   **Craig Adamson**

60049 (Page 138, bottom) is yet another 'tug' still in the EWS maroon and gold livery and makes for a striking sight, atop a rake of 11 'Gondolas' passing Shawford, near Winchester, on 24th June with 6M26, the 08.50 Eastleigh Yard - Stud Farm ballast empties.   **Peter Slater**

60071 *'Ribblehead Viaduct'* (above) crosses the River Don on 19th November 2012 with 6X73, Doncaster - Toton; running as **'X'** due to tilting points carriers on the rear, albeit out of view.

60099 (below) passes three DRS locos (Nos.20312 / 20309 / 47853) stabled at St James Bridge, Doncaster, as it heads north with 'YEA' welded rail carriers bound for York Klondyke. On arrival back at Doncaster Decoy Yard, No.60099 will work 6L84 to Whitemoor and 6E04 return, both departmental 'trips'. DRS are providing traction for many engineer's trains in Yorkshire and the North East of England, hence the presence of DRS locos stabled here - see later on in "LR 2014" for some more images of DRS locos at work on engineer's trains. **Alan Padley (2)**

60045 *'The Permanent Way Institution'* (above) is out today working the Mountsorrel - Doncaster ballast 'trip' (6M22 / 6M23), which can be formed of different types of wagon each day it runs. On 27th April, No.60045 crosses the River Soar at Normanton, Loughborough, with a rake of 'IOA' internationally registered Bogie Ballast wagons, UIC-coded *'Ealnos'*. The train is 6M22, Mountsorrel - Doncaster Virtual Quarry loaded ballast. **Jamie Squibbs**

60039 (below), fresh from overhaul, works 6M23, the 12:57 Doncaster VQ - Mountsorrel on 4th June. The train consists of 15 autoballasters and is passing through East Midlands Parkway station. Ratcliffe-on-Soar power station occupies a prominent position close to junction 24 of the M1, the River Trent and the skyline for many miles around is dominated by its eight cooling towers. **Jamie Squibbs**

6V75

60074 *'Teenage Spirit'* (above) works 6V75, the 09:30 Dee Marsh - Margam steel empties on 20th April and, viewed through a 300mm lens, it is seen passing Meolle Brace, Shrewsbury. With more 'tugs' in traffic, this service is often worked by a Class 60. **Mike Hemming**

60063 (below) waits 'for the road' on Saturday, 27th July, at a busy Hereford with 6V75, the 09:30 Dee Marsh - Margam just as Colas Class 47 No.47749 'Demelza' arrives light engine from Washwood Heath to effect the rescue of No.56094, which had failed earlier in the week. The wagons forming 6M60, the 04:32 Exeter Riverside - Bescot (via Newport ADJ) are stabled with train loco No.66115 out of sight. **Jim Ramsay**

60007 *'The Spirit of Tom Kendell'* (above) is seen on Wednesday, 13th March, working 6V75, Dee Marsh - Margam, heading along the 'Up Relief' line at East Usk, Newport, with an assorted rake of enclosed steel carriers - steel sided 'BYAs' and canvas sided 'IHAs'. The steel trains running between Dee Marsh and Margam often go via Llanwern to attach / detach wagons.

Having arrived at Llanwern, No.60007 (below) has dropped off all of the wagons it came in with and is now heading back the way it came, passing East Usk Junction with just a single loaded coil wagon in tow. The line to the right of the loco leads to Bird Port steel terminal and Uskmouth power station.   **Chris Perkins (2)**

Ebange Steel

60040 *'The Territorial Army Centenary'* (above) passes Kirk Sandall Junction on 11th February with 6O26, the 14:22 Scunthorpe - Dollands Moor 'FIAs' loaded with steel slab bound for Ebange in France. The 60 will hand over to Class 92 No.92030 'Ashford' at Doncaster Belmont Yard, from where the train will proceed under a 4O26 reporting code. The single line on the right of view leads to the Rockware glassworks at Barnby Dun and the 'freight-only' South Yorkshire Joint Line.   **Alan Padley**

Round Oak Steel

60074 *'Teenage Spirit'* (below) passes Coedkernow, near Newport, on 30th January with 6V05, the 10.01 Round Oak -Margam steel empties, as an HST (Nos.43153 / 43194) is about to overtake on the 'Down Main' with 1B31, the 12.15 London Paddington - Cardiff Central.   **Peter Slater**

Bird Port Steel

60020 (above) is seen pushing 6H35, the 09.32 Margam - Bird Port empty steel carriers down the East Usk branch on Tuesday, 5th March, to be loaded with steel from the Bird Port terminal. An air-piped brake van is at the other end of the train leading, which has a pilot man on board to communicate instructions to the driver. There are no run-round facilities at Bird Port. The semaphore signals at East Usk were removed under the Newport signalling renewal scheme which came into effect on Monday, 4th January 2010. East Usk signal box was formally abolished (already fire damaged) and East Usk Yard, plus the Uskmouth branch, now come under the control of the new South Wales Control Centre in Cardiff.   **Chris Perkins**

With loading completed, No.60020 (below) is seen again heading out of the south portal of Newport Old Tunnel approaching Gaer Junction with 6H36, the 14:44 Newport Bird Port - Margam. The other tunnel bore on the left is Newport New Tunnel, which is also known as Hillfield Tunnel.   **Peter Slater**

6V05

60062 (above) heads 6V05, the 10.38 Round Oak - Margam empty steel on 20th August, as it sweeps round the curve above the banks of the River Wye with a lengthy rake of steel carriers; canvas-sided 'IHAs' and telescopic 'BYAs - very nice!

Peter Slater

The 'Twilight Zone'
Humberside Steel

60040
'The Territorial Army Centenary'

Here's the 'tug' (top right), rounding the curve at Hayfield Crossing at 19.45hrs on 8th April with the diverted 6V19, 17:22 Immingham - Margam empty steel.

The train is passing Milepost 114, which is the mileage from Huntingdon South Junction via March, on the Gainsborough to Doncaster main line.

60063 (middle) emerges into the only patch of sunshine, as it approaches the platforms of the former Rotherham Masborough station with 6J94, the 12:09 Hull Hedon Road - Rotherham steel empties.

Masborough was the main railway station for Rotherham from the 1840s, until most of its trains were rerouted via Rotherham Central in 1987; closing in 1988.

60099 (bottom right) is heading another diverted steel service as a result of the Hatfield landslip, this time on 25th April.

No.60099 is passing Auckley on the Doncaster to Gainsborough line with 6E08, the 13:11 Wolverhampton - Immingham steel empties.

Auckley is a village and civil parish about five miles east of Doncaster and is recorded in the Domesday Book of 1086.

Alan Padley (3)

Reminiscences .... No.60001 *'Steadfast'* (above) is seen on the second day (21st March 1991) of Class 60 testing in the Calder Valley, heading west at Hebden Bridge with 6M54, the 09:07 Leeds - Stanlow empty petroleum tanks; Class 37/7 No.37706 is tucked inside for insurance.

Meanwhile, 12-years later, now in EWS livery and renamed, No.60001 *'The Railway Observer'* (below) passes Hambleton West Junction on 5th February 2003 with 6D04, the 11:18 Hull Dairycoates - Rylstone 'Tilcon' empties. Note the elevation of the line in the background, where it crosses the ECML.   **Neil Harvey (2)**

'Tug' Profile

60001

In Traffic
August 1991

Depot Allocation
August 1991	:	Stewarts Lane
March 1997	:	Toton
November 2000	:	Thornaby
May 2004	:	Immingham

Livery
August 1991	:	Two-Tone Grey
?	:	EWS Maroon and Gold (applied between 07/97 and 07/01)
August 2013	:	DBS Red

Names
June 1989	: *Steadfast*
February 2001	: *The Railway Observer*

Withdrawn
March 2006

Reinstated
August 2013

Notes

1. No.60001 carried Trainload Freight Construction sub-sector decals of blue & yellow squares until June 1996.

2. In June 1996, "Rolling Wheels" logo with Mainline branding replace the blue & yellow squares.

3. 'The Railway Observer' naming was seven years to the day since the name was applied to Class 37 No.37890 at Hither Green.

A secondary plate is also carried, which is inscribed:

'The Journal of the Railway Correspondence and Travel Society Founded in 1928

RCTS

www.rcts.org.uk'.

4. No.60001 was stored after a major engine failure, while working one of the Liverpool - Fiddlers Ferry coal circuit diagrams on 24th February 2006.

Two-Tone Grey livery.	Crewe	11th August 1990

EWS Maroon & Gold livery.	Toton	7th April 2007

DBS Red livery.	Toton	28th August 2013

Craig Adamson (3)

Construction Materials

60091 (above) is pictured approaching Uffington signal box on the Peterborough to Syston Junction route leading 6M34, the 12:23 Ferme Park London Concrete - Croft empty 'Bardon' hoppers. These wagons are coded 'JGA' and were built by W H Davis, Shirebrook, in 2005 and are numbered AI27101 - AI27122. **James Welham**

60092 (below) is about to pass under the footbridge at Salfords station on 2nd May with 7O48, Leicester Humberstone Road - Crawley stone; clouds of dust rise into the air from the well filled bogie boxes as the driver piles on the power after a speed check. **Alan Hazelden**

Rare Outings

60074 *'Teenage Spirit'* (above) passes Husborne Crawley on the Bedford - Bletchley (Marston Vale) line with an unusual Friday working of 6H10, the 09:56 Bletchley - Peak Forest. The date is 15th March and the consist is a real assortment of bogie hoppers: 'HOAs', 'IIAs' and ex-RMC 'JGAs'.

60099 (below) makes a very rare appearance for a 'tug' on 16th March when it is seen deputising for the booked DBS Class 66/0 loco passing Oakley, near Bedford, in charge of 6C32, the 07:27 Mountsorrel - Elstow. The consist is mostly 2-axle 'PGA' stone hoppers, which are prefixed REDA in the number range 14501 - 14519 and 14750 - 14839. These wagons are used on aggregate flows out of Mountsorrel to Barham, Broxbourne, Elstow, Kennett, Radlett and Trowse. **Nigel Gibbs (2)**

Industrial Sand
60092

6E88 : A rare visitor for the Goole sand train on Friday, 15th February, is No.60092 (above), which is passing through Whittlesea heading west with 6E88, the 12:39 (MWFO) Middleton Towers - Goole. The sand will be used at the Guardian glass works, one of the world's largest manufacturers of float glass and fabricated glass products. Unfortunately, only the raw materials arrive by rail, the finished products leave by way of the nearby M62 motorway. **Alan Hazelden**

6H93 : On the return working, No.60092 (below) approaches Doncaster station on Saturday, 16th February, whilst working 6H93, the 05:25 Goole - Doncaster Up Decoy. The consist is made up of the unique WBB Minerals branded 'PAA' 2-axle sand hoppers built by W H Davis between 1981-1983. **Jim Ramsay**

Rylstone 'trips'

6D71 : It's a number of years since a Class 60 last worked 6D71 but, on 12th February, No.60020 (above) is unusually seen at the discharge terminal, after arriving with 6D71, the 03:53 Rylstone - Hull Dairycoates. A stanchion of the Humber road bridge can be seen in the background.   **James Skoyles**

6D72 : No.60020 (below) is nearing journey's end with the return 'empties' from Hull, crawling past Skipton Golf Course with 6D72, the 11:32 Hull Dairycoates - Rylstone, formed of 'JGA' covered bogie hoppers, in the number range NACO 19170 - NACO 19199.

Swinden quarry (Rylstone) is on the Skipton to Grassington Line in North Yorkshire (owned by Tarmac, previously Tilcon) and despatches limestone to Hull, Leeds and Redcar. The branch leaves the main line at Skipton North Junction and runs as single track for some eight miles to Rylstone.   **Neil Harvey**

60020 (above) is seen again on 11th February near Embsay with 4D79, the 09:18 Redcar - Rylstone empties, formed of both 'HOA' and 'IIA' bogie hoppers on this occasion. The normal 'COVHOP' hoppers, carkind 'JGA', are working the Hull dairycoates diagram (6D71 / 6D72). **Neil Harvey**

60074 'Teenage Spirit' (below) makes for a cracking composition as it passes Old Denaby on 17th October 2012 with 6Z44, Pendleton - Scunthorpe Ent. Centre empty bogie hoppers, after delivering slag from the steelworks for a construction project. Old Denaby lies in the southern outskirts of Mexborough. **Ross Byers**

Reminiscences .... No.60100 *'Boar of Badenoch'* (above) in two-tone grey livery, albeit with Mainline logo, heads along the South Wales Main Line near Coedkernew on a slightly misty 3rd September 1999 with 6V08, the 05:30 Wolverhampton - Margam steel empties. Judging by the pink stain on the cab roof, it has also been up and down this line at some time on the Port Talbot to Llanwern iron ore trains.　　**Martin Loader**

Meanwhile, now in EWS livery of maroon and gold, No.60100 *'Pride of Acton'* (below) is seen stabled at Bedworth oil terminal (between Nuneaton and Coventry) on 23rd May 2005 after arriving with 6M61, the 03:38 Lindsey - Bedworth loaded petroleum tanks. The consist would be 19 bogies.　　**Craig Adamson**

'Tug' Profile

60100

In Traffic
December 1992

Depot Allocation
December 1992   : Toton
October 1993   : Stewarts Lane
March 1997   : Toton
September 2005   : Immingham

(Above) : No.60100 'Pride of Acton'.   Toton   7th April 2007

Livery
december 1992   : Two-Tone Grey
   Trainload Freight Construction sub-sector decals of blue & yellow squares.
June 1996   : Two-Tone Grey
   "Rolling Wheels" logo with Mainline branding replace the blue & yellow squares.
?   : EWS Maroon and Gold (applied sometime between 2001 - 2003)
August 2013   : DBS Red

Names
December 1992   : *Boar of Badenoch*
June 2003   : *Pride of Acton*

Withdrawn
   : April 2006

Reinstated
   : September 2013

No.60100 (above) now devoid of nameplates, shows off its new coat of DBS corporate red at Toton TMD on 5th October, following its recent overhaul - another 'tug' back on the books! **Craig Adamson (2)**

6A83
60063

While most freight services from South Wales to London and the Home Counties use the direct route via Swindon, some aggregate trains are routed via Bath, Westbury and the 'Berks & Hants' line, such as 6A83, the 12:15 (WFO) Machen Quarry - West Drayton.

On 11th January, No.60063 (above) starts to level off after the 4-mile climb at 1 in 100 out of Severn Tunnel to reach Pilning on 11th January with loaded Hanson branded 'JHA' Bogie Aggregate Hoppers, running as 6A83, the 12.15 Machen Quarry - West Drayton.   **Chris Perkins**

Meanwhile, No.60063 (below) is now approaching Hawkeridge Junction, slowing to take the chord to Heywood Junction to join the 'Berks & Hants' main line, avoiding Westbury station.   **Mark Pike**

Intermodal & Wagonload

Class 60s are not regular performers on Wagonload services, rarer still on Intermodal. They generally turn up as a substitute for a 'shed', or when a 60 is needed to act as 'super shunter' at a yard, such as Eastleigh, Hinksey or Westbury, for example.

6E62 : "Last Rites" .... it's the end of an era, as the highly colourful 'UBC' intermodal (chemical traffic) between Tees Dock and Carlisle runs for the last time on 8th December 2012. No.60091 (above) is 'fixed' to work the train and, after being held at a red signal on the approach to Gateshead Metro Centre, a 'record shot' is grabbed of a lengthy 6E62, the 10:29 Carlisle Yard - Tees Dock intermodal, as it passes Derwent Haugh, near the Metro Centre - 6E62, RIP!   **Martin Cook**

6A58 : 60045 *'The Permanent Way Institution'* (below) passes through Aylesbury on 30th October 2012 running on the Princes Risborough branch with 6A58, the 10:16 Calvert - Northolt empty 'binliner'. The date is 30th October 2012 and this is may have been the last time a 60 worked this service.   **David Stracey**

6V02 : No.60062 (above) passes Brompton foot crossing on the important freight artery which links Teesside with the ECML at Northallerton. The date is 22nd July and the working is 6V02, the 18:38 Tees Yard - Margam, which consists of containerised lime from Thrislington, used to line the blast furnaces at Port Talbot steelworks. Steel is also conveyed on this service. **Ian Ball**

6V51: No.60040 *'The Territorial Army Centenary'* (below) passes through Bristol Temple Meads station on 22nd March in charge of 6V51, the 03:05 (TThO) Warrington Arpley - Portbury Wagonload, formed of empty car carriers. Imported cars go north on 6X52, the 17:33 (TThO) Portbury - Mossend. **Edward Gleed**

6L05 : A rarity indeed .... 60011 (above) a surprise, but welcome, choice for 6L05, 13:58 Wakefield Europort - Felixstowe intermodal on 28th August 2012. It is seen passing Oakenshaw Lane, Wakefield, but No.60011 only works as far as Doncaster. **Neil Harvey**

6V38 : Tata grey liveried No.60099 (below) awaits the road at South Moreton (about a mile east of Didcot) on 14th March with 6V38, the 13:50 Eastleigh Yard - Didcot Yard Wagonload service. The consist is reminiscent of 'Speedlink' services with a combination of vehicles: an intermodal flat, empty car carriers, 2-axle spoil wagons, plus some empty 2-axle fuel oil tanks at the rear of the train. **Steven King**

Solent 'trips'

There are several intermodal / wagonload 'trip' workings between Southampton Western Docks and Eastleigh Yard and, when a Class 60 is at Eastleigh, one can often turn up on these workings.

6B43 : No.60065 *'Spirit of Jaguar'* (above) approaches Mount Pleasant Level Crossing, just south of St. Denys, on 21st August with 6B43, the 09:38 Eastleigh Yard - Southampton Western Docks 'trip'. The service is also being used as a bit of a crew trainer, judging by the number of people in the cab!

6B44 : No.60099 (below) is coming out of the docks at Millbrook on 5th February with 6B44, 12:07 Southampton Western Docks - Eastleigh Yard wagonload 'trip'.

6X44 Vice 6B44

6B44 : No.60045 *'The Permanent Way Institution'* (above) is approaching Southampton Central with 6B44, the 12:07 Southampton Western Docks - Eastleigh Yard on 3rd September, consisting solely of containers.

6X44 : No.60092 (below) is passing through Southampton Central on 23rd April with the same service as that depicted above. However, this time it is running as 6X44 ex-Southampton Western Docks, which is always coded 'X' (out of gauge) when conveying cars, such as on this occasion.   **Mark Pike (4)**

60092

Preston Docks 'Bitumen' traffic : It's a fine day on 3rd June and the sun has got its hat on, just about enough to shine on No.60092 (above), as it tops Copy Pit Summit (749ft) on the Burnley - Todmorden line with 6E32, the 08:55 (MWFO) Preston Docks (Lanfina) - Lindsey bitumen empties. Meanwhile, and a few hours later, No.60092 (below) has the "Dreaming Spires" of Killingholme refinery as a backdrop, nearing the end of its journey heading 6E32 through Brocklesby.

Neil Harvey / Syd Young

The National 'Grid'

Background

1973 : FORTY YEARS AGO, 1973, British Rail decided a new fleet of freight locos was necessary, ostensibly for 'Merry-Go-Round' coal workings to and from coal fired power stations, to replace pairs of Class 20s and Class 47s - enter the Class 56 .....

Brush Traction (Loughborough) tendered for the contract to build 135 new locos, but space constraints at Loughborough works, resulted in the work being sub-contracted to Electroputere in Romania.

1976 : Parts for the locos were shipped out to Electroputere and the first Class 56s were handed over to British Rail on 4th August 1976 at Zeebrugge, Holland.

1977 : No.56006 becomes the first Romanian built loco to enter service on 27th February 1977.

Just 30 of the class were built in Romania. Poor reliability and lengthy periods out of service resulted in BR bringing production back to the UK for the remaining 105 locos: Nos.56031 - 56115 built at BREL Doncaster and Nos. 56116 - 56135 at Crewe.

The End

The days of the 56s were numbered with the introduction of the new GM (General Motors) Class 66 locos, resulting in .....

1998 : Over half of the original fleet are taken out of traffic.

2004 : Only two 56s remained in traffic at the end of March 2004, none by April 2004.

Renaissance

It is somewhat ironic that, for a Class of loco to be deemed 'non-standard' and expensive to maintain by EWS (now DBS), the 56 should now be seeing a new lease of life ....

Timeline

2006 : Jarvis Fastline return Nos.56045, 56124 and 56125 to the mainline in the guise of 56301, 56302 and 56303 respectively.

2007 : Hanson follow suit, resurrecting No.56057 and No.56003 as No.56311 and No.56312.

2009 : Jarvis withdraw their three locos due to a downturn in traffic.
Nos.56301 and 56302 are purchased by the Class 56 group and Edward Stevenson. 56303, 56311 and 56312 now operate under 'Devon & Cornwall Railways' branding.

2012 : Colas Rail return Nos.56094 and 56087 to traffic in June, mainly replacing their Class 66/8s on the Chirk timber flows.

2013 : Colas reactivate Nos.56105 and 56113.
Nos.56078 and 56051 await overhaul and a return to revenue earning service.

"The future's bright" .... certainly 'orange', in many respects, for these fine locos!

Portfolio

With the movements of the very popular Class 56s being closely followed by enthusiasts, *'Loco Review'* features extended coverage of great 'grid' action ....

State of Play

Class 56s 06:00hrs, Wednesday, 2nd January 2013

Number	Pool	Location	Status
COLAS			
56051	COLO	Burton WS	B - Not to be moved, awaiting documentation
56078	COLO	Washwood Heath	D - At TMD awaiting maintenance
56087	COLO	Washwood Heath	X - Exam or repair at depot
56094	COLO	Washwood Heath	N - Normal (available for traffic)
56105	COLO	Washwood Heath	X - Exam or repair at depot
56113	COLO	Washwood Heath	D - At TMD awaiting maintenance
56302	COLO	Washwood Heath	N - Normal (available for traffic)
DCR			
56091	HTLX	Washwood Heath	U - Stored Unserviceable
56103	HTLX	Washwood Heath	U - Stored Unserviceable
56301	HTLX	Washwood Heath	N - Normal (available for traffic)
56303	HTLX	Calvert	N - Normal (available for traffic)
56311	HTLX	Washwood Heath	X - Exam or repair at depot
56312	HTLX	Washwood Heath	N - Normal (available for traffic)

The Chirk 'Logs'

There are currently four services taking timber to the Kronospan works at Chirk and, with the introduction of more Class 56s, Colas Rail have been able to use them on the timber traffic instead of their Class 66/8s.

Let's take a look at '56s' at work on each of these respective flows:

6Z53, 14:41 Teigngrace - Chirk

6Z70, 12:40 Ribblehead - Chirk

6M37, 09:50 Baglan Bay - Chirk

6J37, 12:44 Carlisle Yard - Chirk

56087 (right) :

Carlisle sometimes takes delivery of Devon timber (believed to be a different grade of hardwood) approximately once a month.

In the early hours (02:59hrs), while most of us are fast asleep in bed, the photographer captures a shot of No.56087 on 16th November 2012 as it waits for a path from Carlisle Citadel station with 6Z53, the 14:41 Teigngrace - Carlisle Yard timber.

Fred Kerr

6Z53, 14:41 Teigngrace - Chirk

56094 (above) heads through a snow storm at Pilning on Wednesday, 23rd January, returning to Devon with the empty log carriers from Chirk: 6Z52, the 07:13 Chirk Kronospan - Teigngrace. An unidentified unit descends the 1 in 100 gradient towards Severn Tunnel making its way to Cardiff.　　**Chris Perkins**

No.56094 (below) is seen again one month later on Wednesday, 20th February, standing at Newton Abbot after running round 6Z52, the 17:00 Gloucester New Yard - Teigngrace, with a rake of empty 'KFAs' bound for the loading terminal, just over 2-miles away on the Heathfield branch.　　**Robert Sherwood**

56105

On 11th April, No.56105 (above), has exited Whiteball Tunnel, Marlands, and looks mightily impressive sweeping round the curves with 6Z53, the 14:41 Teigngrace - Chirk 'logs'. The main A38 road linking Taunton and Exeter passes right over the top of the tunnel.   **Peter Slater**

At the time, No.56105 was the latest addition to the Colas fleet of 'grids' and, after making the booked stop, No.56105 (below) sets off from the loop at Sutton Bridge Junction, Shrewsbury, with 6Z53, the 14:41 Teigngrace - Chirk 'logs'. The 'grid' will pass through Shrewsbury station and continue heading north for a further 21 miles to Chirk.   **Mike Hemming**

6Z52 : On 6th February, No.56094 (above) sweeps down off the flyover at Cogload Junction with 6Z52, the 07:13 Chirk Kronospan -Teignspan -Teigngrace empty timber carriers. 56s in Devon - things are looking up!

Peter Slater

6Z70 : On 6th February, having left the loading point at Ribblehead and run round its train at Blea Moor, No.56302 (below) retraces its steps with 6Z70, the 12:40 Ribblehead - Chirk timber.

Fred Kerr

6Z70, 12:40 Ribblehead - Chirk

56302 becomes the first 'grid' to work the loaded timber train from Ribblehead to Chirk on 31st May and here are two more shots to record the event, especially pleasing when the weather on the Settle & Carlisle stays fine.

No.56302 (above) leaves the loading point adjacent to Ribblehead station for the short run to Blea Moor and a reversal, after which No.56302 (below) heads down through Selside Shaw, passing the 'Limestone Pavements', running about three-quarters of an hour early at this point.   **Fred Kerr / Neil Harvey**

6M37, 09:50 Baglan Bay - Chirk

56105 (above) passes Ponthir, near Newport, heading along the "Welsh Marches Route" on 30th April in charge of 6M37, the 16:20 Baglan Bay - Chirk loaded timber destined for the Kronospan MDF plant. Both the Baglan Bay and Teigngrace timber flows came on stream in 2012 - great stuff!   **Peter Slater**

56087 (below) is running 10 minutes early as it passes Sutton Bridge Junction, Shrewsbury, with 6Z50, the 07:13 (MWFO) Chirk - Baglan Bay empty timber carriers on 25th July. The area around Shrewsbury is still blessed with many fine examples of ex-GWR lower quadrant semaphore signals.   **Mike Hemming**

6J37, 12:44 Carlisle Yard - Chirk

56105 (above) roars south through Kirkby Stephen station on 20th April, while working 6J37, the 12:44 Carlisle - Chirk timber. A couple of passengers pass the time with idle chat, waiting patiently for the next Northern Rail service to Carlisle which, based on the signal, will shortly be arriving.   **Steven Brykajlo**

56094 (below) passes Kitchenhill Bridge, a pleasant spot just off Junction 41 of the M6 motorway at Penrith, with 6J37 running 90+ minutes late on 27th October 2012. The stream the 56 is crossing over is the infant River Petteril, which has its source near the small village of Penruddock.   **Guy Houston**

56087 (above) is newly refurbished and repainted. It is heading 6J37 south at Great Strickland in lovely autumn sunshine at 14:15hrs on 17th November 2012, passing Milepost 45 on a gradient of 1 in 125, eight miles of climb before reaching Shap summit. 6J37 can be routed via Shap or the 'S. & C'.   **Guy Houston**

56105 (below) has been routed via the 'S & C' and eases its long train of timber carriers through Long Preston on 20th April in charge of 6J37, the 12:44 Carlisle - Chirk 'logs'. It doesn't get much better than this, a beautiful West Yorkshire setting of luscious green pastures and dry stone walls.   **Richard Armstrong**

"It's a Pair"

56087 + 56105 (above) roar through Buckshaw Parkway station on 14th July with 6C37, the 22:25 Chirk - Carlisle Yard empty timber carriers, diverted off the WCML via Bolton for part of the journey. Buckshaw railway station opened on 3rd October 2011 on the Manchester to Preston Line, built on the site of the former Royal Ordnance Factory (ROF, Chorley), which had a four-platform ROF station halt.

56302 + 56087 (below), meanwhile, approach Euxton Balshaw Lane on 10th June with the loaded service: 6J37, the 12:44 Carlisle Yard - Chirk. The train will run 'under the wires' as far as Warrington, where it will leave the main line and go via Helsby, Chester and Wrexham. **Fred Kerr (2)**

56087 + 56105 (above) are a truly amazing sight, as the pair of Colas 'grids' come off Ribblehead viaduct in glorious sunshine on Friday, 5th July with 6Z70, the 12:40 Ribblehead - Chirk loaded timber. Class 56s have never been common on the 'S & C', let alone a pair working in multiple!   **Martin Cook**

56105 + 56094 (DIT) (below) pass Ruckley on the Shrewsbury - Wolverhampton main line, between Shifnal and Cosford, on 3rd July with 6C37, the 22:25 Chirk - Carlisle Yard. The time is 21:30hrs and the sun has just set, there being just enough light to see the 56s pass the poppy fields. The truncated train is due to No.56094 failing, causing a late arrival at Chirk, and there being insufficient time to unload a full train and get the 'empties' out before the onset of engineering works.   **Mike Hemming**

As well as scheduled WTT work, both Colas Rail and DCR Class 56s are available for work on a 'Spot Hire' basis, providing traction for:

- cover, when other freight operators suffer motive power shortages.
- 'one off' vehicle and 'On Track Plant' moves.
- short term freight contracts, especially scrap metal.

'Spot Hire'

For example, on 18th February, Colas Class 56 No.56302, now devoid of Fastline colours and sporting the orange, yellow and black Colas livery, is rostered to work a special Llanwern - Long Marston - Llanwern move, taking steel wagons in and out of storage. The first leg involves moving steel sided VTG steel-sided 'JSA' steel carriers to Long Marston and returning with the following rake of canvas-sided 'IHAs':

84.4667.049	84.4667.143	84.4667.075	84.4667.086	84.4667.068
84.4667.056	84.4667.060	84.4667.108	84.4667.107	84.4667.105
84.4667.064	84.4667.189	84.4667.104	84.4667.077	84.4667.123

On the outward journey, No.56302 (top) is seen heading the delayed 09.07, Llanwern - Long Marston along the STJ - Gloucester main line at Woolaston, Lydney, with the 'JSAs' in tow.   **Peter Slater**

Photographed from a public footpath crossing, No.56302 (above) passes through the flat landscape of the Vale of Evesham at Bretforton with 6Z37, the 14:55 Long Marston - Llanwern train of 'IHAs', having earlier deposited the 'JSAs' at Long Marston.   **Martin Loader**

56312 (above) is captured passing Rotherham on 6th July with a rare working for a 'grid', taking damaged Class 222 'Meridian' unit No.222101 to Crofton for repair. The train is 5Z56, Derby Etches Park - Crofton and the 'grid' manages to avoid the advancing shadows, at a time when the sun is high in the sky! **Ross Byers**

56311 (below), being the other DCR grey-liveried 'grid', hauls Gresley Pacific 4-6-2 steam loco No.4468 'Mallard' and Class 55 'Deltic' No.55019 'Royal Highland Fusiliers' through Barkston on the ECML as 5Z75, the 10:30 York NRM - Grantham 'Up Sidings'. The locos will go on display at Grantham during the weekend of 7th and 8th September, to form part of the 75th anniversary celebrations when 'Mallard' set the speed record just south of Grantham at Stoke Bank on 3rd July 1938, hitting a speed of 126mph.   **Nigel Gibbs**

On Track Plant & Departmental 'Trips'

56087

During May, Colas 'Grid' No.56087 finds itself working departmental 'trips' in the South East, working off Hoo Junction and Eastleigh.

On 9th May, No.56087 (top left) makes a rare appearance in Kent working 6Z56, Willesden ET - Hoo Junction and is seen passing through Northfleet station moving part of the Kershaw High Output Ballast Cleaner. **Stuart Chapman**

On 13th May, No.56087 (middle) is stabled in the sidings alongside Eastleigh station, pending an overnight engineer's 'trip' (see below) to North Camp. Another 'heritage' loco is also stabled in the shape of BR Green-liveried Class 31/0 No.31190, which is hooked up to 'RailVac' No.9570.9515.001-4.

Overnight, now the 14th, No.56087 (below) has reached its destination and has come to a halt at North Camp station, having arrived with 6C61 rail train. North Camp is located on the Wokingham to Guildford main line.

Simon Howard (2)

56303 (above) is captured in a delightful rural setting at Beambridge, near Wellington, on 11th April with lovely shades of green all around. No.56303 is hauling a single vehicle ('RailVac' No.9570.9515.001-4) and is running as 6Z57, the 09.47 Doncaster Wood Yard - Plymouth Keyham. **Peter Slater**

56302 (below) is tucked in behind DRS Class 57 No.57010, double-heading 6K60, Carlisle Yard - Ayr 'trip' on 4th June, passing Eastriggs on the ex-Glasgow & South Western Railway main line. The train was booked for a pair of Colas Class 47s, but ended up with Colas hiring-in No.57010 to help No.56302. **Guy Houston**

Metal

56094 (above) becomes the first Class 56 to work a revenue earning steel train in South Wales since No.56115 passed this point on the 30th March 2004 with an Orb Steelworks - Llanwern steel 'trip'. On Wednesday, 13th March, No.56094 passes East Usk, Newport, in charge of 6F04, the 14:30 Newport Docks - Llanwern empty steel carriers.

Chris Perkins

On the evening of 26th March, DCR Class 56 No.56311 leads a failed ex-Fertis liveried, and recently reinstated, No.56091 on 6Z69, 20:58 Cardiff Tidal - Chaddesden empty scrap. Unfortunately, 6Z69 only gets as far as Lydney 'Up' Goods Loop and No.56311 works forward as 0Z69, 01:45 Lydney Loop - Washwood Heath, leaving No.56091 (below), and its consist of modified 'JRA' box wagons behind. No.56303 is duly despatched (0Z56) to affect a rescue and the ensemble of No.56303 + No.56091 + 'JRAs' finally leave on 27th March, running as 6Z69, Lydney Loop - Chaddesden.

Jamie Squibbs

56303 + 56301 (above) stand at Chesterfield on 3rd September with a special 6Z56, Stockton - Cardiff Tidal loaded scrap. These services operate under 'STP' arrangements, usually booked on the day of travel, which makes it difficult for enthusiasts to monitor their movements.　　**Mick Tindall**

The biggest rail project in Nottingham for a generation gets under way during July as almost all rail services at Nottingham station are cancelled until the end of August. The work is part of a £100 million project to replace six miles of track around the station and add a new platform. More than 140 signals will also be replaced. Consequently, freight services are being diverted and on 19th August, No.**56094** (below) is seen passing Stamford, Lincolnshire, with the diverted 6E07, 06:00 Washwood Heath - Boston Docks steel empties. The train will reverse at Peterborough and run to Newark to rejoin its booked route. **Nigel Gibbs**

56105 (above) leaves the main line at North Stafford Junction on 26th September while working 6S96, the 12:52 Sinfin - Grangemouth empty aviation fuel tanks. The electricity lines of the national grid are overwhelming as the other 'grid' passes underneath, taking the Crewe line on its long journey north. **Ian Cuthbertson**

56312 'Jeremiah Dixon' (below) approaches Skelton Junction on 27th September with 6Z56, the 10:45 Wolsingham - York Holgate empty 'JRA' bogie box wagons move. The 'grid' is sporting DCR's new corporate grey livery, which is very similar to the old Departmental Grey livery of the '80s and '90s. **Neil Harvey**

Grangemouth Fuel Oil 'Grid'

'Grangemouth tanks'

6L82, Linkswood

6R46, Prestwick

6M85, Sinfin

Colas Rail replaced DBS in May 2012 to provide traction for the Grangemouth aviation fuel oil trains, in the shape of a Class 66/8 loco or the occasional Class 47/7.

However, in August, Colas send Class 56 No.56105 North of the Border as a substitute for a Class 66/8 loco (actually, No.66849) which returns south. The 56 will work the internal aviation fuel oil 'trips' between Grangemouth and Linkswood / Prestwick.

It's 10 years since a 'grid' saw freight service in Scotland and, looking back through the records, it would appear that the last 56 turn was an 'Enterprise' diagram:

4S92, 01:08 Tees Yard - Mossend   **6E89, 19:07 Mossend - Immingham**

After arriving from the south at the weekend, and after a couple of false starts, it's all systems go for a Class 56 to start working regular freight trains in Scotland again. No.56105 (top) passes through Camelon on 23rd August in the gloom at 07:55hrs with 6L82, the 07:42 Grangemouth - Linkswood (for RAF Leuchars airbase), formed of 2-axle BP fuel tanks.   **Guy Houston**

Fortunately, it's better weather five days later when No.56105 (above) is seen passing through Alloa station while working 6N72, the 14:48 Linkswood - Grangemouth empty fuel tanks.   **Steven Brykajlo**

Back to the 23rd August, the weather is still awful, but No.56105 (above) is nonetheless a cracking sight as it screams through the murk just south of Gleneagles, viewed from the Glen Devon road with 6L82 Grangemouth - Linkswood oil tanks for RAF Leuchars.   **Guy Houston**

(Overleaf) : On the following day, No.56105 (Page 188) makes a colourful addition at Culross; it's high tide and the 'grid' casts a modest reflection on the waters of the Firth of Forth, as it returns to base after delivering an additional trainload of aviation fuel to Linkswood.   **Alastair Blackwood**

On 14th September, Network Rail need to move wagons to Mossend for weekend engineering work and Colas provide traction for a special Saturday working from Carlisle. In lovely weather, No.56105 (page 189) powers 6Z56, Carlisle - Mossend at Crawford Viaduct, running on time and sounding great.   **Guy Houston**

Meanwhile, on 4th September, No.56105 (below) is seen passing Cupar with 6N72, a mere six miles into its journey back to Grangemouth after delivering the fuel oil for RAF Leauchars.   **Jim Ramsay**

State of Play

DRS Class 37s 06:00hrs, Wednesday, 2nd January 2013

No.	Pool	Location	Number	Pool	Location
37038	XHNC	Crewe Gresty Bridge	37059	XHSS	Barrow Hill
37069	XHSS	Crewe Gresty Bridge	37087	XHSS	Barrow Hill
37194	XHNC	Carlisle Kingmoor	37218	XHNC	Crewe Gresty Bridge
37229	XHSS	Crewe Gresty Bridge	37259	XHNC	Hither Green (working 2Q35)
37261	XHNC	Crewe Gresty Bridge	37401	XHHP	Barrow Hill
37402	XHHP	Barrow Hill	37405	XHHP	Barrow Hill
37409	XHAC	Derby RTC	37410	XHHP	Carlisle Kingmoor
37411	XHHP	Derby RTC	37419	XHAC	Under 'GENIUS' Control
37422	XHHP	Crewe Gresty Bridge	37423	XHAC	Derby RTC
37425	XHAC	Crewe Gresty Bridge	37510	XHSS	Barrow Hill
37601	XHNC	Carlisle Kingmoor	37602	XHNC	Hither Green
37603	XHNC	Crewe Gresty Bridge	37604	XHNC	Crewe Gresty Bridge
37605	XHNC	Hither Green (2Q35)	37606	XHNC	Inverness
37607	XHNC	Crewe Gresty Bridge	37608	XHNC	Sellafield
37609	XHNC	Crewe Gresty Bridge	37610	XHNC	Crewe CLS
37611	XHNC	Sellafield	37612	XHNC	Sellafield
37667	XHNC	Sellafield	37682	XHNC	Derby RTC
37683	XHHP	Off T.O.P.S.	37688	XHNC	Sellafield

37419 'Carl Haviland' (above) stands for a brief moment at Perth on 21st December 2012 before being unhooked from the business end of 1M16, the 20:44 Inverness - London Euston sleeper, at 23:45hrs; the 37 provided for ETH purposes at Inverness behind Class 67 No.67007 up front. The train continues without No.37419 from Perth to Edinburgh Waverley, with the train loco (No.67007) being unable to provide ETH for the remainder of the journey, so some cold punters onboard! **Guy Houston**

West Coast DRS Intermodal

37610 'T.S. (Ted) Cassady' + 37602 (above) are turned out on 20th June to work 4M44, the 08:47 Mossend - Daventry intermodal, substituting for the 'booked' Class 66/4 loco. The pair are seen in fine fettle 'growling' nicely on the West Coast Main Line as they pass Newton, Johnstonebridge, near Lockerbie. **Ian Ball**

(Overleaf) : 37606 passes under the splendid canopy of Carlisle Citadel station on 16th November 2012 with a lightweight and very late running 4M30, the 19:54 Grangemouth - Daventry. Citadel station was built in 1847, in a neo-Tudor style to the designs of William Tite. **Fred Kerr**

37607 + 37610 'T.S. (Ted) Cassady' (below) look impressive as they sweep into view at Fiddler's Gill, Carluke, on 10th June with 6M82, the 15:18 Coatbridge - Daventry intermodal, with yet another Class 66/4 substitution, but who cares, it's powerful stuff! **Kenny Marrs**

Top 'n' Tail Class 37s

Class 37s vice Class 153 units - 25th August

DRS Class 37/4s, No.37405 and No.37425 work south from Carlisle Kingmoor to Crewe on Wednesday, 21st August, with three coaches in tow - a TSO / TSO / BSK formation.

The loco and coaches are for a shuttle service planned for Sunday, 25th August, substituting for Class 153s, and will bring the rare sight of loco-hauled trains to the Derby - Stoke - Crewe route. These services will be top and tailed.

East Midlands Trains have a staff shortage and cannot cover 'rest day' working on this route. So, instead of cancelling the services, EMT have hired-in another Train Operator to cover five services, as outlined opposite.

The 37s and stock will be running to Class 153 timings between Crewe and Derby and, after the final train service, it's ECS back to Crewe.

Selective Images :

5Z37 : It's all over .... No.37425 and No.37405 (above) top 'n' tail 5Z37, Derby - Crewe CS and approach Uttoxeter on Monday, 26th August, taking the stock back home after the Class 153 replacement service comes to an end.   **Mick Tindall**

1K02 : As No.37405 leads over the level crossing at Bramshall, No.37425 'Concrete Bob/Sir Robert McAlpine' (top right) brings up the rear of 1K02, the 15:05 Crewe - Derby. No.37425 was re-named 'Sir Robert McAlpine / Concrete Bob' at the DRS Carlisle Kingmoor Open Day on 17th August. No.37425 transferred to Glasgow Eastfield TMD in February 1986 and was originally named 'Sir Robert McAlpine/Concrete Bob' in October the same year. It stayed in Scotland until January 1989, when it moved south to Cardiff Canton, assigned to the Freight Aggregates sector.

1K05 : No.37425 (bottom right) is seen arriving at Stoke-on-Trent with 1K05, the 16:38 Derby - Crewe; these services are well patronised by enthusiasts with over 300 allegedly packed into the three coach formation on this particular working!   **Mark Walker (2)**

1K14 : The last leg of the day .... No.37405 (Previous Page) finds itself leading as it stands at Crewe, prior to departure with 1K14, the 21:16 Crewe - Derby. It's seven years since No.37405 last saw passenger service: 12th July 2006, working a sleeper 'portion' into Edinburgh.   **Mick Tindall**

1K02

Crewe	15:05
Alsager	15:14 -15:14
Kidsgrove	15:21 - 15:21
Longport	15:26 - 15:26
Stoke-on-Trent	15:31 - 15:32
Longton	15:37 - 15:38
Blythe Bridge	15:43 - 15:44
Uttoxeter	15:56 - 15:56
Tutbury & Hatton	16:05 - 16:06
Derby	**16:21**

1K05

Derby	16:38
Tutbury & Hatton	16:52 - 16:52
Uttoxeter	17:02 - 17:03
Blythe Bridge	17:17 - 17:17
Longton	17:22 - 17:23
Stoke-on-Trent	17:30 - 17:31
Longport	17:36 - 17:36
Kidsgrove	17:42 - 17:43
Alsager	17:46 - 17:47
Crewe	**17:57**

1K08

Crewe	18:09
Alsager	18:18 - 18:18
Kidsgrove	18:23 - 18:23
Longport	18:29 - 18:29
Stoke-on-Trent	18:34 - 18:36
Longton	18:41 - 18:42
Blythe Bridge	18:47 - 18:48
Uttoxeter	18:59 - 19:00
Tutbury & Hatton	19:09 - 19:09
Derby	**19:24**

1K11

Derby	19:41
Tutbury & Hatton	19:55 - 19:55
Uttoxeter	20:05 - 20:06
Blythe Bridge	20:20 - 20:20
Longton	20:25 - 20:26
Stoke-on-Trent	20:33 - 20:34
Longport	20:39 - 20:39
Kidsgrove	20:45 - 20:46
Alsager	20:49 - 20:50
Crewe	**21:00**

1K14

Crewe	21:16
Alsager	21:24 - 2125
Kidsgrove	21:29 - 2130
Longport	21:35 - 2136
Stoke-on-Trent	21:40 - 2142
Longton	21:47 - 2148
Blythe Bridge	21:53 - 2154
Uttoxeter	22:05 - 2206
Tutbury & Hatton	22:15 - 2215
Derby	**22:30**

Class 37 Fact File

37405

Last timetabled passenger working	: 12th July 2006
1B26, 06:45 Carstairs - Edinburgh	: 28.75 miles
Allocated to XHAC - DRS Class 37/47 ETS	: 28th June 2013
25th August Mileage (50.88 x 3)	: 152.64 miles

37425

Last timetabled passenger working	: 24th June 2012
1G95, 18:15 Lowestoft - Norwich	: 23.54 miles
Allocated to XHAC - DRS Class 37/47 ETS	: 13th June 2012
25th August Mileage (50.88 x 2)	: 101.76 miles

North of the Border

37218 + 37194

6S99, Sellafield - Georgemas Junction

On 15th April, Nos.37218 and 37194 (above) are seen sweeping round the curve on the approach to Gleneagles with 6S99, the 05:30 Sellafield - Georgemas Junction "flasks" - a single Magnox flask on a Flatrol 'FNA' wagon. Meanwhile, earlier in their journey, the 37s (below) look like they have passed underneath the Falkirk Wheel at Larbert Junction, the point at which the lines from Grangemouth and Edinburgh join. Apart from intermodal traffic, this flask train is the only DRS-hauled freight service to be seen on this route and a 37 is a most welcome distraction to the usual diet of Class 66s.

37605 (above) heads 1Q23, Inverness - Mossend Network Rail test train on the approach to Stirling station, passing Stirling North signal box on 29th April with No.37218 on the rear. There are two signal boxes at Stirling and it remains to be seen how long the semaphore signals will remain here, as work is underway to install Multiple Aspect Signalling in the area. The line can be seen above the first vehicle, which is used by Glasgow Queen St. - Stirling - Alloa passenger trains and Longannet power station coal trains.

37606 (below) is seen on 10th May, unusually deputising for a Colas Class 66/8 loco on 6R46, the 07:11 Grangemouth - Prestwick fuel oil tanks, waiting to leave Fouldubs Junction, Grangemouth. Colas 66/8 loco No.66847 fails after leaving Grangemouth and DRS are asked to supply a replacement loco; No.37606 is duly summoned, seen here six hours later. **Guy Houston (4)**

West Highland 'Tractor'

37419

Week commencing 18th February, heralds the start of ballast drops on the West Highland Line. DRS Class 37/4 No.37419 'Carl Haviland 1954 - 2012' (above) is seen tooting its way heading west at Crowwood Grange, Stepps, on the outskirts of Glasgow with 6K60, Mossend - Fort William, bound for the WHL.   **Guy Houston**

No.37419 (below) stands in Oban station on the evening of 20th February, just like old times, having arrived with 6K60, Carlisle - Oban loaded autoballasters. Later in the evening, the train carries out a number of ballast drops between Oban and Connel Ferry. This is the first Class 37 hauled ballast train to reach Oban since 2004. The impressive McCaig's Folly overlooks the town in the background.   **Steven Brykajlo**

On 28th February, No.37419 (above) has reached Corrour Summit with 6K61, Fort William - Bridge of Orchy, after dropping ballast alongside Loch Treig, between Tulloch and Corrour. The 37 was meant to shunt 6K61 out the way at Corrour to allow a passenger service to pass but, as it turns out, the driver receives the token early for the run to Rannoch and so the shunting manouevre was not needed.

Later the same day, the sun makes a brief appearance when No.37419 (below) stands at Bridge of Orchy with 6K61, Bridge of Orchy - Mossend ballast empties, shortly before departing over one hour early!

No.37419 was transferred from DBS to DRS in August 2011, repainted into DRS Livery at Barrow Hill in December 2011 and allocated to the XHAC (Class 37/47 ETS) Pool in May 2012. **Guy Houston (2)**

37423 'Spirit of the Lakes' + 37409 'Lord Hinton TMD' (above) are captured in a very lucky patch of morning sunshine, storming north on the WCML towards Wandel on 24th June, while working 6K40, the 07:15 Carlisle Yard - Inverness Rose Street ballast. Meanwhile, some eight hours further into their journey, Nos.37423 + 37409 (below) pass Killiekrankie, north of Pitlochry, on the Highland Line with 6K40 ballast.

Steven Brykajlo / David Stracey.

E.C.S. Moves

37518 **'Fort William'** (above) passes through the Fens on 11th March at Ramsey Road, Whittlesea, having just come out of a snow shower to find a patch of sun. The 'tractor' is working 5Z55, the 08:35 Sheringham NNR - Castleton, returning 5MT 4-6-0 No.45407 'The Lancashire Fusilier' and BR 4-6-2 Pacific No.70000 'Britannia', plus support coaches, from the North Norfolk Railway steam gala.   **Nigel Gibbs**

37261 **+** 47501 (below) in top 'n' tail mode, power away from North Stafford Junction on 8th February working 5Z30, Derby - Crewe CS, formed of a solitary Northern Belle coach, No.3273. The train is passing over the B5008 level crossing with a backdrop of five cooling towers, the remnants of long-closed Willington power station. Peregrine Falcons have been known to nest in the impregnable towers!   **Jamie Squibbs**

Departmental Moves

37608 + 37218 (above) have the throttle wide open as they accelerate northwards at Colton Junction on 29th January with 6T67, the 09:40 Doncaster - York empty Continuous Welded Rail train, which also has a Railhead Treatment set on the rear hitching a ride back to York. **Mark Walker**

37667 (below) ambles through the station platforms of the former Rotherham Masborough station on 8th February with 6Z37, Etruria - Doncaster Decoy, which involves the movement of two 'ZOA' Kirow KRC250UK Heavy Duty Diesel Hydraulic Cranes. The train has come via Sheffield Midland, while the far two lines in view are the 'Old Road' (freight only), which go via Treeton and Barrow Hill. The 'Old Road' joins up again with the Sheffield Midland main line at Tapton Junction, Chesterfield. **Alan Padley**

37516

WCRC 'Snow Patrol'

This loco was acquired by WCRC (West Coast Railway Company) from DB Schenker in February 2009 and returned to traffic in June the same year. During February and March 2013, it is hired out (with other WCRC locos) to Network Rail on snowplough duties. On 27th March, No.37516 + Class 47/7 No.47760 (above) 'plough through' Dove Holes station during a blizzard heading for Buxton with 1Z99, Carlisle - Buxton.

After a two hour layover at Buxton, No.37516 + No.47760 (below) get to work clearing snow from the Hindlow branch and the duo are seen passing Harpur Hill with 1Z99, Hindlow - Buxton.   **Mick Tindall (2)**

There's excitement in Kent too, when WCRC locos turn up for the latest round of snow trains. On 13th March, with only a trace of snow left on the ground, Class 47/0 No.47245 + No.37516 (above) are working Snow & Ice Treatment Train (SITT)) 8Y98, Tonbridge - Tonbridge, seen through the fields at Farningham. It's been commented on many times before that the WCRC livery in dull weather is tricky, but this one seems to work fairly well set against the green field behind. **Ian Cuthbertson**

On 21st February, No.37516 + Class 33/0 No.33029 (below) approach High Brooms on the Hastings Line taking the (SITT)) back to Tonbridge, having been down to St Leonards for fuel. **Alan Hazelden**

37688 'Kingmoor TMD' + 37402 (above) top 'n' tail two Network Rail test train vehicles as they cross Bebside Viaduct on 30th August while working a circular 1Q13, 09:57 Heaton – Heaton, via Morpeth. This viaduct, also known as the 'Black Bridge', spans the River Blyth, linking Bebside and Bedlington. It was built by the LNER in 1930, to replace an old wooden structure, 80 feet high and 770 feet long. **Martin Cook**

37602 + 37607 (above) are seen in top 'n' tail mode, nearing the end of their journey on 26th February passing Wool (Dorset) with 6Z41, the 03:02 Crewe CS – Winfrith Sidings, the first visit to this location since Nos.37611 + 20310 on 10th September 1999. Winfrith was a United Kingdom Atomic Energy Authority site, opening in 1958 and used for nuclear reactor research and development. The last reactor was shut down in 1995, although decommissioning will not finish until 2018.

Mark Pike

DRS Bound

37703 (L25)   **37714 (L26)**   **37716 (L23)**   **37718 (L22)**

Of the six Class 37s which returned to the UK from Spain last September, it is pleasing to report four are to find work again with Direct Rail Services. These four locos are being moved by road to Barrow Hill (Nos.37703 and 37714) and Derby RVEL (Nos.37716 and 37718) for overhaul.

These two images show the start of the move away from Dollands Moor on 12th August by low-loader: Nos.L26/37714 plus No.L25/37703 (above) and No.L22/37718 (below). The locos are at Junction 9 of the M20 motorway, starting out on their long and slow journey north.

The loco livery is similar in design to EWS, which is the original GIF base livery (with 'L' number identity), since gaining Continental Rail branding following their acquisition of GIF.   **Michael Wright (2)**

A Long Stretch

37688 'Kingmoor TMD' + 37402 are on an extensive tour of Humberside and the North East of England. Brightening up a gloomy start to 12th September in North Humberside here, at Melton Lane one mile west of Ferriby station, No.37688 (above) leads 1Q13, the 05:48 Doncaster - Tees Yard Network Rail test train.

Meanwhile, now heading along the 'Up fast', No.37402 (below) leads 1Q13 past Welton level crossing as a threatening sky heralds an oncoming rainstorm.

The longest and flattest stretch of straight railway line in Britain runs from Selby Swing Bridge to just short of Ferriby - over 20 miles - so straight, you can practically see the curvature of the Earth! Another interesting statistic is that between Gilberdyke Junction and Ferriby (9 miles) there are seven signal boxes, which control some excellent examples of LNER upper quadrant semaphore signals. **Syd Young (2)**

State of Play

Class 20s 06:00hrs, Wednesday, 2nd January 2013

Number	DRS Pool	Location	Status	Working
20301	XHSS	Eastleigh	X	
20302	XHSS	Eastleigh	X	
20303	XHSS	Eastleigh	X	
20304	XHSS	Eastleigh	X	
20305	XHSS	Carlisle Kingmoor	T	
20306	XHSS	Barrow Hill	T	
20307	XHSS	Carlisle Kingmoor	T	
20308	XHNC	Crewe Gresty Bridge	N	
20309	XHSS	Carlisle Kingmoor	X	
20310	XHSS	Carlisle Kingmoor	T	
20312	XHNC	Carlisle Kingmoor	T	
20313	XHSS	Carlisle Kingmoor	T	
20315	XHSS	Carlisle Kingmoor	T	

Number	GBRf Pool	Location	Status	Working
20096	GBEE	Peterborough	N	6M21, Peterborough - Old Dalby
20107	GBEE	Barrow Hill	N	
20142	GBEE	West Ruislip	N	
20189	GBEE	West Ruislip	N	
20227	GBEE	West Ruislip	N	
20311	GBEE	Barrow Hill	N	
20314	GBEE	Peterborough	N	6M21, Peterborough - Old Dalby
20901	GBEE	Peterborough	N	6M21, Peterborough - Old Dalby
20905	GBEE	Peterborough	N	6M21, Peterborough - Old Dalby

Somewhat of an unusual sight is observed on the West Coast Main Line on 4th June. Instead of the routine transit of nuclear flasks on 'FNA' Flatrol Bogie Wagons, Class 20s No.20305 + No.20309 (above) top 'n' tail a special 6Z45, 15:18 Sellafield - Crewe service, consisting of 'PFA' 2-axle Container Flats, which carry low level waste containers. These particular wagons are in the number range DRSL92703 - DRSL92856 and the train is passing Red Bank, north of Warrington. **Neil Harvey**

Departmental Excursions

Network Rail call upon DRS to provide motive power for engineer's trains in Yorkshire, Humberside and the North East of England.

It would also seem that DRS are keen to extend these duties even further by taking over other departmental turns from DBS, notably the out & back 'trips' between Crewe Basford Hall and Carlisle Yard (6C02 / 6K05), for example.

From where will these locos come, for all these new turns?

(Selective Images)

(Top Right) : Having arrived at Thorne Junction 20 minutes earlier than booked, it's only a 'grab' shot to record the passing of this triple-header on 25th April. Nos.20302 + 20304 + 20312 take the single line spur off the Hatfield & Stainforth main line at Thorne Junction with empty 'Falcon' ballast wagons heading for Goole. The train is routed back to Doncaster via Goole, Snaith, Hensall and Knottingley.   **Alan Padley**

(Overleaf)

(Page 212) : Does motive power get much rarer than this on the East Coast Main Line in the North East? The same trio of locos are seen again, this time Nos.20312 + 20304 + 20302 shatter the peace and quiet as they thrash away from Ferryhill with 6Z30, the 13:04 Ferryhill South Junction - Doncaster 'Up' Decoy on 19th April, consisting of continuous welded rail carriers.   **Martin Cook**

(Page 213) : It seems strange seeing 20s top 'n' tailing a freight train, which does not involve nuclear flasks. However, this pleasant sight sees Nos.20305 'top' and 20302 'tail' 6Z33, Haydon Bridge - Doncaster Marshgate engineer's train passing Hag Lane, Raskelf, on the East Coast Main Line.   **Ian Ball**

(Below) : On 25th March, Nos.20308 + 20312 pass Bessacarr in charge of 6Z37, Scunthorpe Trent Sidings - York Holgate RDT, which has been diverted via Barnetby - Brigg - Gainsborough - Bessacarr, as a result of the diversions put in place following the Hatfield landslip in February.   **Alan Padley**

'S Stock' Moves

20096 + 20107 (above) have passed underneath the M6 Motorway flyover approaching Washwood Heath, Birmingham, on 26th June with 7X09, the 11:42 Old Dalby - Amersham. The train will proceed via Landor Street Junction - Bordesley Junction - Tyseley - Leamington Spa - Banbury to Aynho Junction, where it will head onto the Chiltern Main Line for the remainder of the journey. **David Weake**

20142 + 20189 + 20901 + 201107 and 20314 + 20311 (below) are a truly colourful and impressive sight, whistling merrily through Crown Lakes Country Park in Yaxley (just South of Peterborough) on 19th August working 6M10, the 09:48 Peterborough GB - West Ruislip barrier wagon positioning move. This section of the ECML runs as double track for six miles between Holme and Fletton Junction. **Nigel Gibbs**

20311 + 20314 (above) are passing Saltley on 6th August with 7X10, the 02:27 Amersham - Derby Litchurch Lane taking a unit back to Derby for rectification work. The pair of 20s on the rear are Nos.20107 and 20901; a Class 66/0 is waiting to come off the stabling point and the football stadium in the background is St. Andrews, home to Birmingham City.

20905 + 20901 (below) look impressive in their new GBRf livery as they approach Bordesley Junction, Birmingham, on 9th July with 7X10, the 02:27 Amersham - Derby Litchurch Lane, with Nos.20096 and 20107 out of sight on the rear .... another unit going back to Derby for rectification work!   **David Weake (2)**

'R.S.G.' Out to Play Again

Following a successful outing in 2011 working the Alcan alumina 'trips' between North Blyth and Lynemouth, GBRf look to Class 55 No.55022 'Royal Scots Grey' again to help out with a loco shortage.

The 'Deltic' is on hire to GBRf who need extra traction for a contract to move Scottish EMUs for refurbishment.

These EMUs are having their inner gangways replaced, plus the fitting of new seat covers and floors.

55022 'Royal Scots Grey'

Glasgow Cross : It's back to work again in May for the Deltic and, on 3rd May, No.55022 (top) passes through the City of Glasgow at Glasgow Cross with a unit move (5N11) from Shields Electric Depot bound for Glasgow Works (St. Rollox). **Alastair Blackwood**

Eastfield : On the 4th May, No.55022 'Royal Scots Grey' (above) sits in the sunshine prior to departing Eastfield loop with 5Z55, Glasgow works - Yoker with translator vans for use in another unit move (6Z53) later in the day conveying a Class 334 EMU to Kilmarnock for refurbishment. **Guy Houston**

6Z53, Yoker CS - Kilmarnock

Jordanhill : Although the sun is out at Eastfield for the barrier move to Yoker, it was not to be when No.55022 hooked up to the stock to form 6Z53, Yoker CS - Kilmarnock. In rapidly fading light, No.55022 (above) is seen shortly after departure passing Jordanhill with the barrier vehicles, translator vans, plus the Class 334 EMU, No.334030.   **Guy Houston**

Kilmarnock : Having arrived at Kilmarnock and run round the train, No.55022 (below) prepares to depart from Platform 3 with 6Z53 and complete the short journey from here to Brodie's works.

The refurbishment of the ScotRail Class 334 EMUs (No. range 334001 - 334040) is being undertaken between 2012 - 2014 at Brodie's, while other EMUs needing refurbishment go to Railcare at Springburn or at Wabtec Rail in Doncaster.   **Alastair Blackwood**

Class 37 & 47 Cab Ends, Kingsbury

37678, Kingsbury

37884 / 37800, Kingsbury

58022, Crewe

56074, Kingsbury

20306 and Class 37s, Rotherham

Classic Traction Graveyard
Images : Craig Adamson

37670, Kingsbury

47710, Kingsbury

47536 & 37370, Rotherham

56049, Kingsbury

45 Years Ago

11th August 1968

The 1T57 'Fifteen Guinea Special' was the last main-line passenger train to be hauled by steam locomotive power on British Railways on 11 August 1968 before the introduction of a steam ban that started the following day. It was a special excursion train organised for the occasion from Liverpool via Manchester to Carlisle and back, and was pulled by four different steam locomotives in turn during the four legs of the journey (with two engines sharing the third leg).

The Fifteen Guinea Special was so named because of the high price of tickets. 15 guineas = £15 15s 0d in pre-decimal British currency and this price had been inflated due to the high demand to travel on the last BR steam-hauled mainline train.

Based on the Retail Price Index (August 1968 : 16.61 / August 2013 : 249.70) that same ticket would now cost a staggering £249.70!

11th August 1968

1T57, Liverpool Lime Street - Carlisle - Liverpool Lime Street

Miles	Location	Booked Time	Booked Time
00.00	**Liverpool Lime Street**	**09:10d**	**19.50a**
05.50	Huyton	09:22	19:40
14.58	Earlestown	09:54	19:28
31.50	**Manchester Victoria**	**10:36 - 11:06** (L)	**18:48 - 19:02** (L)
42.20	Bolton	11:27	18:30
51.77	Darwen	12:01	18:12
56.09	Blackburn	12:08 - 12:16 (W)	17:58 - 18:04 (W)
67.07	Clitheroe	12:34	17:39
80.35	Hellifield	12:54	17:22
83.60	Settle Jct	12:58	17:18
97.54	Blea Moor	13:24 - 13:29 (W)	16:58 - 17:04 (W)
108.75	Ais Gill	13:45 - 14:05	16:44
126.37	Appleby West	14:23	16:14
156.40	**Carlisle Citadel**	**14:56** (L)	**15:30**

Traction :

45110	Liverpool Lime Street - Huyton - Earlestown - Eccles - Deal Street - Manchester Victoria
70013	Manchester Victoria - Bolton - Darwen - Blackburn - Clitheroe - Hellifield - Appleby - Carlisle
44781 & 44871	Carlisle - Manchester Victoria (reverse of outward route)
45110	Manchester Victoria - Liverpool Lime Street (reverse of outward route)

Notes : (L) = Loco Change   (W) = Stops for water

To commemorate this momentous day, two specials run in August;

 7th August : "Fifteen Guineas Fellsman" (Lancaster - Preston - Settle & Carlisle - Carlisle and return)

11th August : "Fifteen Guinea Special" (exact rerun of 11th August 1968, 1T57 special train)

7th August 1968

The weather on 11th August 2013 is not as favourable as the 7th, which restricts photographic coverage of the second train so, to commemorate the 45th Anniversary, a photographic offering from the 7th is included. Hundreds of photographers line the route and they are not disappointed.

As for myself, I was sitting comfortably on board with my wife, in an ex-Manchester Pullman coach, enjoying cream of asparagus soup followed by roast chicken, as the two locos stormed up the climb to Ais Gill on the return journey - a superb experience all round!

7th August 2013

		1Z52, 07:08 Lancaster - Carlisle	1Z53, 15:34 Carlisle - Lancaster
Miles	**Location**	**Booked Time**	**Booked Time**
00.00	**Lancaster**	**07:08d**	**20:41**
20.78	Preston	07:37 - 08:05	19:48 - 20:05
33.09	Blackburn	08:28 - 08:32	19:19 - 19:22
43.73	Clitheroe	08:58 - 09:03	18:48 - 18:52
57.21	Hellifield GL	09:48 - 10:44 **(W)**	17:55 - 18:15 **(W)**
58.56	Long Preston	10:47 - 10:51	17:50 - 17:52
60.57	Settle Jct	10:54	17:46
76.80	Blea Moor	11:20	17:28
82.68	Garsdale	11:31	17:17
92.72	Kirkby Stephen	11:44	17:00
103.37	Appleby	11:57 - 12:15 **(W)**	16:24 - 16:40 **(W)**
133.40	**Carlisle**	**12:58**	**15:34**

Traction : 2 x **LMS Stanier Class 5 4-6-0 'Black Five' Nos.44932 & 45231**

7th August : selective images

Nos.44932 + 45231 'The Sherwood Forester' (above) blast past Milepost 260 towards Ais Gill Summit with the return 'Fifteen Guinea Fellsman'. An absolutely stunning performance by the 'Black 5s' and a wonderful sight to behold - roll on the 50th Anniversary!   **Neil Harvey**

(Page 222) : The two 'Black 5s' are seen on the outward journey taking a breather as they pass the site of Garsdale troughs with the Lancaster - Carlisle 'Fifteen Guinea Fellsman'.   **Neil Harvey**

(Page 223) : Nos.44932 and 45231 'The Sherwood Forester' put on an absolutely blistering display as they storm past Angerholme on the climb to Ais Gill summit with 1Z53, the 15:34 Carlisle - Lancaster, running as '1T57' - 45 years to the week since steam ended on British Railways.   **Mark Walker**

Contributors

56303 + 56091 lead 56312 + 56301 (above) and four 'JRA' bogie box wagons pas Eldon Lane, Shildon, on 14th September with 6Z58, Wolsingham - Rotherham Masborough, destined for Washwood Heath. No.56312 sports the new DCR grey corporate livery and has been named 'Jeremiah Dixon, son of County Durham surveyor at the Mason-Dixon Line, USA'. Four different liveried 'grids' in one train - WOW!   **Ian Ball**